PRACTICE BOOK

Grade 2

Macmillan McGraw-Hill

New York • Farmington

Macmillan/McGraw-Hill

A Division of The **McGraw·Hill** Companies

Copyright © 1997 Macmillan/McGraw-Hill, a Division of the Educational and Professional Publishing Group of The McGraw-Hill Companies, Inc.

All rights reserved. No part of this book may be reproduced or transmitted in any form or by any means, electronic or mechanical, including photocopying, recording, or by any information storage and retrieval system without permission in writing from the publisher.

Macmillan/McGraw-Hill
1221 Avenue of the Americas
New York, New York 10020

Printed in the United States of America

ISBN 0-02-181186-5 / 2

6 7 8 9   D B H   02 01 00 99 98

CONTENTS

LEVEL 6

UNIT 1: FAMILY FUN

LEVEL 6

UNIT 2: EUREKA!

UNIT 3: BETTER TOGETHER

UNIT 1: PENPALS

Dear Daddy . . .

Best Wishes, Ed

Puff . . . Flash . . . Bang!

Angel Child, Dragon Child

UNIT 2: HAND IN HAND

UNIT 3: NATURE'S WAY

WHAT IS THE MEANING OF THIS!

Read each sentence. Look at the underlined word. Draw a line from the word to what it is.

1. I picked the <u>ginger</u> in the garden.

2. The <u>chimpanzee</u> climbed the tree.

3. Jim plans to take a trip to <u>Hawaii</u>.

4. Kara painted her room <u>lavender</u>.

5. Dad made <u>bento</u> for dinner.

6. Do you see the bird's nest in the <u>jacaranda</u>?

a. an animal

b. a plant

c. a place

d. a food

e. a tree

f. a color

Macmillan/McGraw-Hill

6 Level 6/Unit 1
CONTEXT CLUES: Unfamiliar Words

Extension: Give the children other words; have them look up the definition in the dictionary and write a sentence that gives a clue to its meaning.

23

Bit, Bat, Bet, But

rut

Change the vowel in each word to make a word that rhymes with **rut**. Then use one of the words to complete each group.

| shot | cat | bet | hat |

Things that _____

scissors

ax

knife

Kinds of shelter

cabin

tent

_____

Things that open and _____

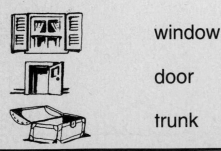

window

door

trunk

B words

ball

bed

_____

24   **Extension:** Have children use each -ut word in a sentence.

Level 6/Unit 1
Short Vowels and Phonograms /u/ -ut

4

Macmillan/McGraw-Hill

WHAT IS YOUR BEST GUESS?

Read the story. Write the answers to the questions.

Alex has a job helping Mr. Jones deliver papers every day. His friend, Jay, needs a job. He wants to earn some money to buy his mom a birthday gift. Mr. Jones needs just one person to help him. Alex cannot give Jay the money, but he can give him something else for a short time. With a smile, Alex goes to talk to Mr. Jones.

1. What do you think Alex will say to Mr. Jones?

   _____

   _____

2. What do you know that helps you make your prediction?

   _____

   _____

3. What do you think Jay will do to get some money?

   _____

   _____

4. What do you think Jay will say to Alex?

   _____

   _____

4

Level 6/Unit 1
Make, Confirm or Revise Predictions

Extension: Ask children to use their predictions to make up the ending to the story.

25

Macmillan/McGraw-Hill

DEAR JOURNAL

Imagine that you are Luka. You are writing in your journal.
Write about how you felt on these two days.

Dear Journal,

Today Tutu gave me a white quilt. I felt sad and angry

because _____

_____

_____

_____

Dear Journal,

Today Tutu gave me a quilted lei. I felt happy

because _____

_____

_____

_____

Extension: Ask children to choose another day in the story and tell what they would write in their journals if they were Luka. Ask how their feelings compare to their feelings on these two days.

Level 6/Unit 1
Comparison and Contrast

2

Macmillan/McGraw-Hill

CHECK YOUR FACTS

Think about "Luka's Quilt." Put a ✔ by each sentence that tells about something you read in the story.

_____ Tutu and Luka live in Hawaii.

_____ Luka wants to make Tutu a quilt.

_____ Luka likes colorful flowers.

_____ Tutu tells Luka to choose many colors for her quilt.

_____ Luka is sad when she first sees the quilt that Tutu made for her.

_____ Tutu calls a truce and takes Luka to Lei Day.

_____ Luka decides to make her lei only one color.

_____ Luka and Tutu are still angry with each other after Lei Day.

_____ Luka's lei gives Tutu a colorful idea.

_____ Now Luka likes both her green and white quilt and her quilted lei.

10   Level 6/Unit 1
Story Comprehension

Extension: Ask children to talk about special times they have spent with their grandparents or older friends.

27

Macmillan/McGraw-Hill

KITE FLYING TIME

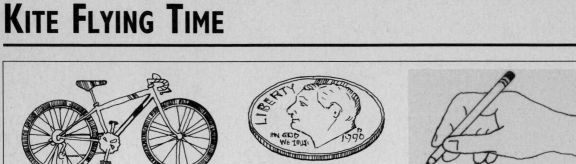

| bike | dime | write |

Use each word below to write about what is happening in the picture.

| like | Mike | time | white | kite |

_____

_____

_____

_____

_____

Extension: Have children make a three-column chart and list words with the **i** sound spelled *-ike, -ime, -ite*.

Level 6/Unit 1

Long Vowels and Phonograms /ī/ *-ike,*

-ime, -ite

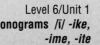

5

Macmillan/McGraw-Hill

WRITE ON!

Circle the word that completes the sentence. Then write the word.

1. Laura's _____ is very big and pretty.

   best   short   bedroom   _____

2. The fish swim _____ the green leaves.

   choose   between   shoe   _____

3. My new _____ are warm.

   pajamas   jump   bird   _____

4. Danny will go _____ to eat.

   downstairs   apple   hat   _____

5. Sometimes it is hard to fall _____ .

   cat   ball   asleep   _____

6. Mother will carry the new baby _____.

   cold   carefully   daddy   _____

7. Their class is _____ .

   rattle   time   upstairs   _____

8. Brian will _____ the books home.

   room   door   carry   _____

Macmillan/McGraw-Hill

Extension: Have children draw the inside of a house that has two floors. Have them label the upstairs and downstairs and tell what rooms can be found there.

WHO HID BEHIND THE BIG TREE?

Mike h**id** behind the b**ig** tree!

Circle the word that answers the riddle. Then write the word.

1. This can happen to cars on ice.	skid sky ski	_____
2. This is what you put on top of a pot.	let led lid	_____
3. This is another way to say "child."	kit kid kite	_____
4. This is a farm animal who likes mud.	pig peg pen	_____

Extension: Have children write a short story about a pig and a kid. Tell children to underline all the words they use that rhyme with **pig** and **kid**.

30

Level 6/Unit 1
Short Vowels and Phonograms /i/ -id, -ig

Macmillan/McGraw-Hill

PREDICT THE FUTURE

Read each story. Write the answers to the questions.

A. The large mother dog saw her puppy walk onto the ice. The ice was very thin. The mother dog got up and stepped onto the ice.

1. What do you think will happen next?

_____

_____

2. What information helps you make your prediction?

_____

_____

B. Ben was carrying two large bags of trash to the end of the driveway. The bags blocked his view of the skateboard that was in his path. He started running to the garbage truck.

1. What do you think will happen to Ben?

_____

2. What information helps you make your prediction?

_____

4 Level 6/Unit 1
Make, Confirm, or Revise Predictions **Extension:** Ask children to use their predictions and make up endings
to each of the stories on this page. 31

Macmillan/McGraw-Hill

NUMBER, PLEASE!

Read the events from "Carry Go Bring Come." Number each set of events to show the order in which they happened.

A. _____ Leon carries a pink flower upstairs.

_____ Leon is fast asleep.

_____ Grandma wakes up Leon.

_____ Leon carries a flower and a veil to his grandma.

_____ Leon carries a flower, a veil, and a pair of blue shoes to Marlene.

B. _____ The women see Leon looking like a bride.

_____ Everyone runs to the stairs.

_____ Everyone takes her things from Leon.

_____ Leon jumps back into bed.

_____ Leon shouts for help.

Extension: Ask children to retell the story using sequence words like *first, then,* and *last.*

ORGANIZE INFORMATION: Sequence of Events

Level 6/Unit 1

Macmillan/McGraw-Hill

UPSTAIRS DOWNSTAIRS

Think about the house in "Carry Go Bring Come." Where do you find the people in the story? Draw a line to match the name with the place.

I. Mother   was upstairs helping her sister.

2. Grandma   was upstairs getting dressed for her wedding.

3. Marcia   was busy working downstairs.

4. Marlene   was upstairs taking care of her daughters.

5. Leon   was carrying things upstairs and downstairs.

Macmillan/McGraw-Hill

5   Level 6/Unit 1
ORGANIZE INFORMATION: Spatial Relationships

Extension: Have children draw pictures to show the things each character asked Leon to carry.

33

STOP AT THE STORE

We **st**opped at the grocery **st**ore.

Write the word that names the picture.

1. stair
   star
   scare

2. stage
   shark
   state

3. stone
   stove
   soap

4. stick
   sack
   stack

5. tuck
   stuck
   stick

6. story
   sore
   storm

Extension: Have children brainstorm a list of words that begin with consonant blend **st** and then write a sentence using as many of the words as they can.

34

Level 6/Unit 1
Consonant Blends /st/ *st*
6

Macmillan/McGraw-Hill

TELL ME AGAIN!

Think about the story "Carry Go Bring Come."
Then fill in the chart below.

I. Main character (who): _____

_____

2. Problem: The women in his family keep asking him ___

_____

_____

_____

3. What happens: Leon ends up holding so many things

_____

_____

4. Outcome: The women come running and _____

_____

_____

_____

Macmillan/McGraw-Hill

Extension: Ask children to work in groups of three and retell the
beginning, middle, and end of this story. Each child should tell
one part.

35

READ ON

Think about the part of "Carry Go Bring Come" when Leon shouted, "Help!" Then answer each question. Use a complete sentence.

1. What had Leon done right before this part of the story?

_____

_____

_____

2. What did Leon look like?

_____

_____

3. What happened next?

_____

_____

_____

4. Why was this part of the story important?

_____

_____

_____

36
Extension: Ask children to draw a picture of their favorite part of this story. Have them share their picture and tell what it is about.

Level 6/Unit 1
Story Comprehension
4

Macmillan/McGraw-Hill

WHAT A DAY!

 I had to w**ait** an hour tod**ay**.

Write a word from the box to complete each rhyme.

| bait | gray | wait | tray |

1. Hurry up, please. It is a quarter to **eight**. Today is the big day. I can hardly

   _____!

2. I went fishing today with my friend **Nate**. Not a fish did we catch, but they ate all our

   _____!

3. If it is supposed to be a bright, sunny **day**, then why is the sky all cloudy and

   _____?

4. "Oh, no!" yelled **Fay**. "I tripped and dropped the

   _____."

4 Level 6/Unit 1
Long Vowels and Phonograms
/ā/ -ait, -ay

Extension: Have children think of words that rhyme with **wait** and **day** and then write a rhyme.

37

Macmillan/McGraw-Hill

UNIT VOCABULARY REVIEW

Look at each group of words. Underline the word your teacher says.

1. bedroom	2. floppy	3. middle	4. bring
beating	disappear	search	truce
awful	fireplace	rattling	brushed
5. quilt	6. shoe	7. dreams	8. forever
pajamas	spider	decided	forget
curly	space	downstairs	fur
9. asleep	10. whole	11. island	12. different
angry	woods	ladder	garden
awake	worry	soft	straight
13. share	14. paint	15. careful	16. carry
short	pajamas	rattle	carefully
stormy	socks	awful	careful
17. mother	18. choose	19. between	20. picture
father	chew	before	purred
grandmother	clothes	beat	past

38 **Extension:** Have each child look up a different word in the dictionary to find its meaning. Students can share the words and their meanings.

Level 6/Unit 1
Unit Vocabulary Review
 20

Macmillan/McGraw-Hill

THE SUN IS ALWAYS SHINING SOMEWHERE

Match each question with the word that answers it. Write the letter of the answer on the line.

_____ 1. What is the sun doing, even on a cloudy day?

a. happen

_____ 2. What do you do when someone asks a question?

b. important

_____ 3. What is the name of the planet we live on?

c. shining

_____ 4. What do you call something you really need to know?

d. Earth

_____ 5. What can fly across the country in about five hours?

e. pretend

_____ 6. What do you do when you make believe?

f. answer

_____ 7. What does something have to do to take place?

g. sunlight

_____ 8. What shines down from the sky on a day with no clouds?

h. airplane

Macmillan/McGraw-Hill

Level 6/Unit 2
Selection Vocabulary

Extension: Have children research and list all the things that need sunlight to grow.

39

PICTURE THIS!

Read each sentence. Look for clues in the picture.
Then circle YES or NO.

1. The building is on fire.   YES   NO

2. The firefighter is in a fire truck.   YES   NO

3. Water is coming out of the hose.   YES   NO

4. The firefighter is wearing boots.   YES   NO

5. The building has only one window.   YES   NO

6. The firefighter is standing on a ladder.   YES   NO

Extension: Ask children to add something to the picture on this page, and then ask someone to say what they see in the picture.

Level 6/Unit 2
ORGANIZE INFORMATION:
Use Photographs/Art   6

Macmillan/McGraw-Hill

HATS OFF TO THE KING AND QUEEN

Read the story. Then underline the answer to complete each sentence.

The king had a beautiful gold crown that he wore every day. It had red rubies and white diamonds all around it.

The queen had a beautiful gold crown, too. Her crown also had red rubies and white diamonds.

"I'm glad my crown is not as large as your crown," said the queen.

"Why?" asked the king.

"It would be so heavy that my head would hurt!" said the queen.

1. Both crowns were _____ .

   a. the same size

   b. gold

   c. little

2. Both crowns had _____ .

   a. red rubies and white diamonds

   b. red rubies only

   c. white diamonds only

3. The king's crown was different from the queen's crown because _____ .

   a. it was gold

   b. it was bigger

   c. it was smaller

4. The queen liked her crown better because _____ .

   a. it had pearls

   b. it was pretty

   c. it was lighter

4

Level 6/Unit 2

ORGANIZE INFORMATION: Comparison and Contrast

Extension: Ask children to compare and contrast how they and a friend are alike and different.

41

Macmillan/McGraw-Hill

WHAT'S THE BIG IDEA?

Read each story. Underline the answers to the questions.

Ladybugs are insects that are important to farmers and gardeners. Ladybugs eat the tiny insects that eat the leaves of plants. This allows the plants to grow big and strong. Some farmers welcome the orange and black ladybugs. Using ladybugs is better than using spray.

1. What is the main idea?
   a. Ladybugs live in gardens.
   b. Ladybugs are important insects.
   c. Ladybugs like farmers.

2. What do ladybugs eat?
   a. They eat healthy plants.
   b. They eat orange and black spray.
   b. They eat tiny insects.

Jill always likes helping her dad work in his wood shop. She sweeps the wood chips from the floor and stacks the new boards in straight piles. Sometimes her dad lets her use a hammer to pound nails into the wooden toys he makes. That is her favorite thing to do.

3. What is the main idea?
   a. Jill makes toys.
   b. Jill likes wood.
   c. Jill likes to help in the wood shop.

4. What does Jill like to do most?
   a. She likes to pound nails with a hammer.
   b. She likes to sweep the floor.
   c. She likes to stack boards.

Extension: Ask children to identify the details that support each main idea.

Macmillan/McGraw-Hill

THE DAYS ARE GROWING SHORTER

You can use words such as **bigger**, **brighter**, and **closer** to compare. Use the word ending **-er** to compare two people, places, or things.

The sun looks bigg**er** and bright**er** than other stars because it is clos**er** to Earth.

Read each sentence in the paragraph. Write the word that completes it.

It is only six o'clock, yet the sky is _____ than

dark   darker

it was this time a week ago. It is also _____ than

cool   cooler

it was. I've noticed that there are _____ leaves on our

few   fewer

trees than there were yesterday. It is very _____ that

clear   clearer

winter is on the way. Soon the days will be much _____

short   shorter

than the nights. Winter always seems _____, but I do

long   longer

not mind because I get to snowboard and ski.

Extension: Have children add **-er** to *small, slow, new, quick, green,* and *fresh* and then use each in a sentence to compare two people, places, or things.

43

Macmillan/McGraw-Hill

CLIMBING HIGH

Look at the pictures. Choose the words from the box that name the pictures. Use the words to complete the puzzle.

clam	clear	clothes	clock	clap

Across:

2.

4.

Down:

1.

3.

4.

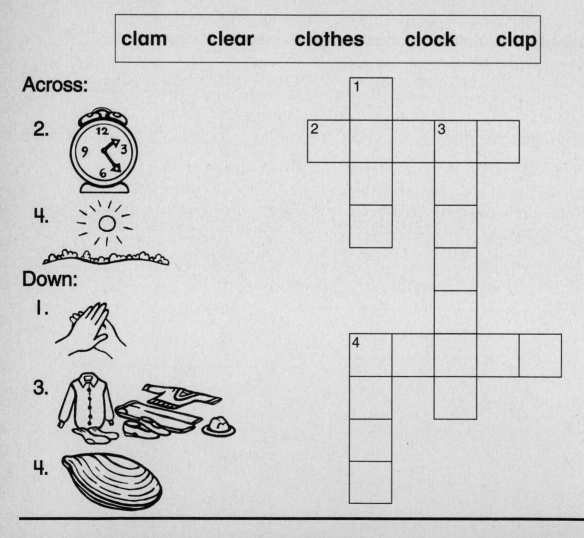

Extension: Have children brainstorm a list of words that begin with **cl** and then work in pairs or small groups to create crossword puzzles.

Level 6/Unit 2
Consonant Blends /kl/ *cl*

Macmillan/McGraw-Hill

Name: _____   Date: _____

SOUP'S ON

Read the story. Number the pictures to show the order in which they happened in the story.

    Grandpa Jake makes the best vegetable soup. First, he boils water in a big pot. Then, he peels carrots and puts them in the pot. Next, he adds corn and green beans. After that, he cuts up potatoes and places them in with everything else to cook. Finally, he adds his own special spices to the soup. My favorite part is eating the soup with fresh bread!

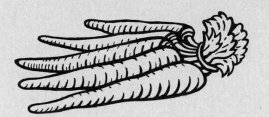

___

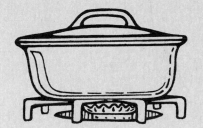

___

___

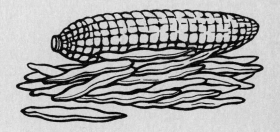

___

___

___

Macmillan/McGraw-Hill

Level 6/Unit 2
ORGANIZE INFORMATION:
Steps in a Process

Extension: Ask children to name the steps they take to make their favorite food. Discuss what would happen if they forgot a step or made it in the wrong order.

SUNNY SIDE UP

Imagine that you are writing to your pen pal. You are writing a letter telling what you have learned about the sun.

Dear _____ ,

Today at school we read a story about the sun. Did you

know that people and animals need the sun to

_____ and _____ ?

We also learned that the sun is a _____

that looks very big because it is _____

_____ .

Did you know that the sun is always shining somewhere?

This is because _____

_____ .

Write back to me soon!

Your friend,

_____

46   **Extension:** Ask children to summarize a story they have just read.

Level 6/Unit 2
Summarize   5

Macmillan/McGraw-Hill

TELL THE TRUTH

Read each sentence. Write the word that will make each sentence a true statement.

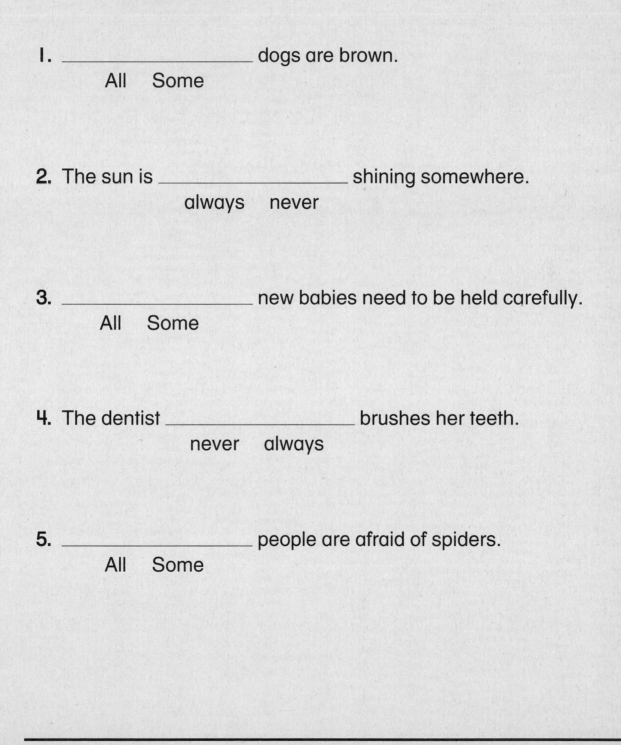

1. _____ dogs are brown.

   All   Some

2. The sun is _____ shining somewhere.

   always   never

3. _____ new babies need to be held carefully.

   All   Some

4. The dentist _____ brushes her teeth.

   never   always

5. _____ people are afraid of spiders.

   All   Some

5   Level 6/Unit 2
Form Generalizations

Extension: Encourage children to use prior knowledge to form other generalizations.

47

Macmillan/McGraw-Hill

MY, MIGHT, MICE

| cry | right | price |

Circle the word that answers the riddle. Then write the word.

1. This is something to eat.

_____

    rice   rise   right

2. This warms the earth.

_____

    sky   sunlight   sight

3. This is what you shouldn't do.

_____

    light   fly   fight

4. This is what something costs.

_____

    price   pies   mice

5. This is an insect with wings.

_____

    fry   fight   fly

6. This is where you see the stars.

_____

    sky   sight   sly

Extension: Have children make a chart of words with /ī/ spelled -y, -ight, and -ice. Then encourage them to create their own riddles for classmates to answer.

Level 6/Unit 2
Long Vowels and Phonograms /ī/-y, -ight, -ice

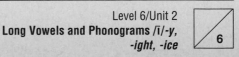

6

Macmillan/McGraw-Hill

FUN IN THE SUN

Think about "The Sun Is Always Shining Somewhere."
Answer each question. Use a complete sentence.

1. How does the sun help people, animals, and plants?

_____

_____

_____

2. Why does the sun look larger than the other stars in the sky?

_____

_____

_____

3. Why can't you see the sun at night?

_____

_____

_____

4. What do you think our world would be like without the sun?

_____

_____

4 Level 6/Unit 2
Story Comprehension

Extension: Ask children to name their favorite activity to do when the sun is shining.

49

CAR MARK

There is a **mark** on my **car**.

Use one of the following words to complete each rhyme.

jar	bark	star	dark

1. "Please don't cry," said **Clark**.

   "There's nothing to fear.

   It's only the _____."

2. Can you tell me how **far**

   I'd have to travel

   to reach the nearest _____?

3. I once had a dog whose name was **Spark**.

   When he saw the moon,

   he started to _____.

4. While unloading the **car**,

   I dropped the bag

   and broke the jam _____ .

Macmillan/McGraw-Hill

50

Extension: Have children use pairs of words that rhyme with **mark** or
car to make up their own rhymes.

Level 6/Unit 2
Variant Vowels and Phonograms /är/
-ark, -ar

4

Name: _____ Date: _____

WILLIE'S NOT THE HUGGING KIND

strong	busy	kitchen	rushing
either	safe	quick	grabbed

Read the story. Choose a word from the box to complete each sentence. Write the word in the sentence. Then reread the story to check your answers.

Lee and Kendra were _____ in the

_____ getting a snack. Dad was in the backyard

making sure their little brother was _____ on the

swing set. Lee was not very hungry, so he took an orange. Kendra

wasn't hungry _____, so she ate some grapes.

They were _____ because the bus would be

there any minute. Today was the big soccer game, and they had

to be on time. While they ate their snack, they talked about how

_____ and _____ they hoped

their team would be.

As the children raced out the door, Lee _____

the soccer ball.

"Good luck!" called Dad.

Level 6/Unit 2
Selection Vocabulary

Macmillan/McGraw-Hill

Extension: Have children use some or all of the vocabulary words to write another story. Encourage children to share their stories with each other.

HUG OR HUT

hug

rut

Write the word that names the picture.

1.

hug
bag
bug

_____

2.

rug
rag
rut

_____

3.

chug
cut
coat

_____

4.

hug
nut
hut

_____

5.

dog
dug
bug

_____

6.

nut
net
shut

_____

Extension: Have children write a sentence using as many words that rhyme with **hug** or **hut** as they can.

Macmillan/McGraw-Hill

WORK CLUES

Read each group of sentences. Fill in the circle by the word that belongs in the blank.

1. Ross and Kate had to do their Saturday morning jobs. They started in the _____ where they swept the floor and washed the breakfast dishes.

   ○ bedroom   ○ kitchen   ○ stove

2. Ross and Kate moved to the living room. They found bread crumbs on the carpet. Ross thought it would be a good idea to _____ the crumbs up.

   ○ vacuum   ○ shake   ○ break

3. After they were done in the house, the children headed for the _____. Dad had moved the car out that morning so they could clean.

   ○ yard   ○ tree house   ○ garage

4. As Kate was reaching for a rag, she knocked over a can of _____. The black greasy liquid spilled all over the front of Ross's shirt.

   ○ oil   ○ water   ○ juice

5. Ross changed his shirt and looked at Kate. He said, "I guess we are not done yet! Now we have to get some soap powder and do the _____."

   ○ dishes   ○ laundry   ○ painting

Macmillan/McGraw-Hill

Level 6/Unit 2
CONTEXT CLUES: Unfamiliar Words

Extension: Ask children to name the clues they found in each exercise that helped them make their word choices.

53

A Squirrel by the Stream

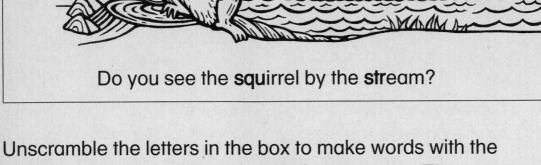

Do you see the **squ**irrel by the **str**eam?

Unscramble the letters in the box to make words with the same beginning sounds as **squirrel** and **stream.** Then use the words to finish the sentences.

squimr	aistrght	gnistr	srtnog	aresqu	quseeez

1. A _____ has four equal sides.

2. You have to be _____ to lift 200 pounds.

3. Do you _____ the toothpaste tube in the middle?

4. You can use _____ to tie the pile of newspapers.

5. The worm will _____ in your hand to get free.

6. My grandma always says to sit up _____ and tall.

54 **Extension:** Have children write silly sentences using as many words that begin like **squirrel** and **stream** as they can.

Level 6/Unit 2
Consonant Blends /skw/*squ*, /str/*str*   6

Macmillan/McGraw-Hill

Give Me a Hug

Read or reread "Willie's Not the Hugging Kind." Write
the name of each character below. Then write how they
each feel about giving hugs.

Macmillan/McGraw-Hill

4

Level 6/Unit 2
ANALYZE STORY ELEMENTS: Character, Plot

Extension: Ask children to tell which one of these characters they are
most like when it comes to hugging.

55

HAPPY ENDINGS

Word endings tell you when an action is taking place.

Rose know**s** how to ice skate.

Rose is teach**ing** Willie how to ice skate.

Willie learn**ed** how to ice skate.

Circle the word that completes the sentence. Then write the word.

1. Max _____ his backpack and ran for the school bus.   _____

   grabs   grabbing   grabbed

2. Our dog _____ everytime he hears thunder.   _____

   barks   barking   barked

3. Megan is _____ an apple pie for dessert.   _____

   bakes   baking   baked

4. Rose _____ to leave for the library right now.   _____

   needs   needing   needed

5. The baby is _____ to walk and talk.   _____

   learns   learning   learned

6. Yesterday, Jan _____ over an hour for the bus.   _____

   waits   waiting   waited

Extension: Have children make three-column charts for verbs ending with *-s, -ed,* and *-ing* and then list the verbs they find in "Willie's Not the Hugging Kind" on their charts.

Level 6/Unit 2
Inflectional Endings *-ing, -s, -ed*

6

Macmillan/McGraw-Hill

JUST BECAUSE

Match the beginning of each sentence with its ending. Write the letter of the answer on the line.

_____ 1. Jack needed to buy a gift

_____ 2. Joe looked in his book bag

_____ 3. Bill couldn't reach the plate

_____ 4. John washed his hands

_____ 5. Kay turned on the computer

_____ 6. Sue's baby brother was crying

_____ 7. Lilly's dog was sick

_____ 8. There was snow on the sidewalk

a. because it was on the top shelf.

b. so she took it to the vet.

c. because it was his sister's birthday.

d. so Alex shoveled a path.

e. because he was going to cook dinner.

f. so she could type a letter.

g. because he needed to find his library book.

h. so she gave him a bottle.

Macmillan/McGraw-Hill

Level 6/Unit 2
ORGANIZE INFORMATION:
Cause and Effect

Extension: Ask children to suggest other sentences that contain the words **so** and **because**.

WHERE AM I?

Read the riddles. Then write the place name that solves each riddle.

1. I watch the monkeys in their cage. Then I visit the seals in their pool. Where am I?

   _____

2. When the bell rings, I sit down. I look in my desk and take out my reading book. Where am I?

   _____

3. I feed peanuts to the squirrels. I watch the children on the swings. Then I sit on a bench and eat lunch. Where am I?

   _____

4. When the lights go down, I can only whisper. Everyone is eating popcorn and watching the show. Where am I?

   _____

5. I jump in the water and swim to the side. The lifeguard waves to me. Where am I?

   _____

58 **Extension:** Ask children to identify specific clues that helped them answer each riddle.

Level 6/Unit 2
Make Inferences

5

Macmillan/McGraw-Hill

WHO NEEDS A HUG?

Think about "Willie's Not the Hugging Kind." Who said each sentence? Circle the answer.

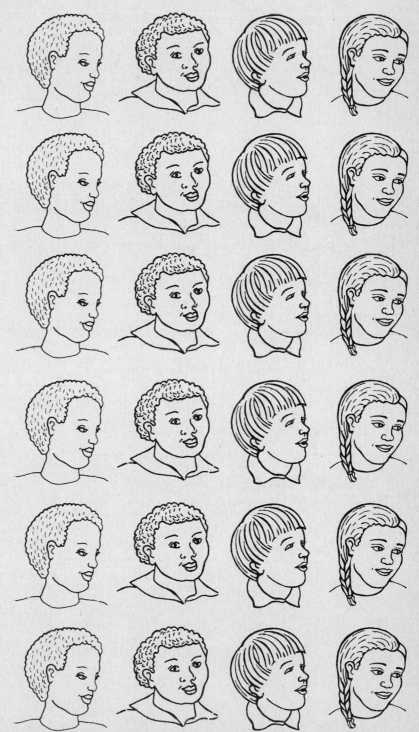

1. "You're just not the hugging kind."

2. "What did you do that for? Man, that's silly."

3. "Help! I'm being mugged! Help!"

4. "What a smelly old bear! I wouldn't hug that old thing for a hundred dollars!"

5. "It's them that don't get hugging who think it's silly."

6. "I think you're what's silly."

6

Level 6/Unit 2
Story Comprehension

Extension: Ask children to read these story quotes aloud using the expression of the character who is saying it.

59

Macmillan/McGraw-Hill

How Does It End?

Rose rode her bike all the way home.

Name the picture. Circle the word that rhymes.
Then write the word.

1. hose   code   home   _____

2. home   rose   toad   _____

3. rode   those   home   _____

4. Rome   rode   chose   _____

5. code   home   nose   _____

6. home   hole   those   _____

Extension: Have children write sentences using rhyming pairs of words from the page.

Level 6/Unit 2
Long Vowels and Phonograms /ō/ *-ode, -ose, -ome*

6

Macmillan/McGraw-Hill

NINE-IN-ONE, GRR! GRR!

Circle the word that answers the riddle. Then write the word on the line.

1. Trees and plants are found here.

   fast   sky   forests   _____

2. I am the opposite of tame.

   wild   wish   middle   _____

3. I am a sound a tiger has made.

   talked   growled   laughed   _____

4. I am sad and by myself.

   lonely   likely   pretty   _____

5. I am the opposite of remember.

   skip   forget   chose   _____

6. I am the far side of a place.

   pretend   father   beyond   _____

7. I am the pattern on a zebra.

   circle   square   striped   _____

8. A teacher did this to teach
   you about something.

   exit   explained   island   _____

Macmillan/McGraw-Hill

8 | Level 6/Unit 2
Selection Vocabulary

Extension: Have children use other words from "Nine-in-One, Grr! Grr!" to make riddles.

61

SWEETS AND THINGS

The str**eam** is thr**ee** f**eet** deep.

In the word box, add **eet** to **gr** and **sw**. Add **ee** to **tr**. Add **eam** to **cr**. Then use the new words in the chart.

| gr_____ | sw_____ | tr_____ | cr_____ |

Parts of a _____	Things that are _____
branches	sugar
leaves	honey
trunk	candy
Things made from _____	**Words used to** _____ **others**
cheese	Hello!
butter	Hi!
ice cream	Good Morning!

Extension: Have children create categories for these words: knee, three, bee, beet, feet, street, stream, team.

Level 6/Unit 2
Long Vowels and Phonograms: /ē/ -ee,
-eet, -eam

4

Macmillan/McGraw-Hill

CAREFUL AND QUICKLY

A suffix is an ending that you can add to certain words. Knowing what a suffix means can help you to figure out what a word means.

Be care**ful**!   Run quick**ly**!

The suffix **-ful** means "full of," so **careful** means "full of care." The suffix **-ly** means "in a certain way," so **quickly** means "in a quick way."

Underline the words that end with **-ly** and **-ful** and circle the suffixes. Below, write what each word means.

A storm was coming, so Luisa and I ran all the way home. We made it home safely, but my sister was still fearful. I tried to be cheerful and brave, even though I was scared, too. Lightning flashed brightly across the sky and thunder rumbled loudly overhead. We were thankful when the storm ended.

1. _____   2. _____

3. _____   4. _____

5. _____   6. _____

Macmillan/McGraw-Hill

Level 6/Unit 2
Suffixes: *-ful, -ly*

Extension: Have children suggest other words to which they can add the endings *-ful* and *-ly*. Encourage children to use the words in sentences.

12

What Is in the Pot?

Jane is making a p**ot** of soup.

Use each word in the box to write about what is happening in the picture below. Underline the words.

spot	lot	hot	pot	not

_____

_____

_____

_____

_____

_____

64

Extension: Make a large pot using construction paper, and place it on the bulletin board. Have children fill it with words that contain /o/-*ot* that have been cut out from newspapers and magazines.

Level 6/Unit 2
Short Vowels and Phonograms: /o/ -ot
5

Macmillan/McGraw-Hill

TIGER TRIP

In the story "Nine-In-One, Grr! Grr!" Tiger travels to see Shao. Read the words in the box. Use these words to write what Tiger sees on her trip.

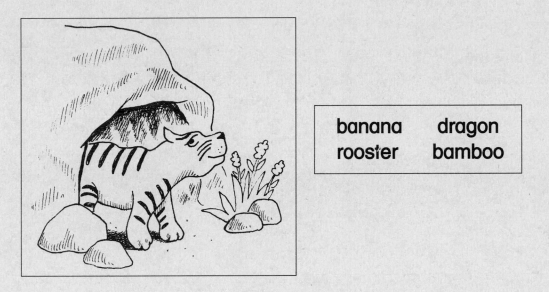

banana	dragon
rooster	bamboo

As Tiger walked up to the sky, she saw forests of striped

_____ and wild _____ trees.

She also saw plants curved like _____ tail

feathers. Tiger walked over rocks that were shaped like a

sleeping _____.

Macmillan/McGraw-Hill

4 Level 6/Unit 2
ANALYZE STORY ELEMENTS: Setting

Extension: Ask children to draw a picture of something Tiger saw on her trip to see Shao.

65

TIGER TALES

A **cause** is the reason why something happens.
An **effect** is what happens.

Cause	**Effect**
Tiger wonders how many cubs she will have each year.	Tiger decides to visit Shao to learn the answer.

Read each cause. Then write its effect.

Cause

Tiger travels to the sky and speaks to Shao.

Effect

_____

_____

Tiger worries that she won't remember what Shao told her.

_____

_____

Bird doesn't want Tiger to have nine cubs each year.

_____

_____

Tiger sings the song "One-in-Nine, Grr! Grr!"

_____

_____

Macmillan/McGraw-Hill

---

66 **Extension:** Sing Tiger's song using different numbers, and ask children what effect it would have on both Tiger and Bird.

Level 6/Unit 2
ORGANIZE INFORMATION:
Cause and Effect

 4

GREAT GRADE

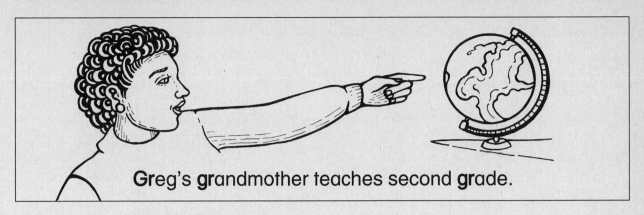

Greg's **gr**andmother teaches second **gr**ade.

Name each picture. Unscramble the letters to make a word that rhymes. Then write the word.

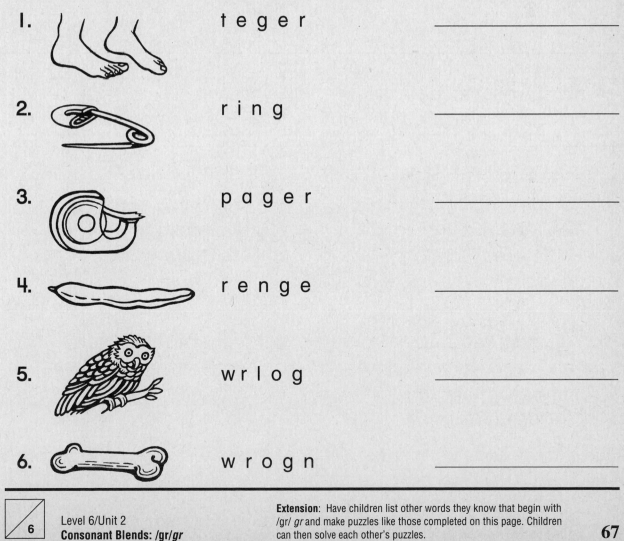

1.   t e g e r   _____

2.   r i n g   _____

3.   p a g e r   _____

4.   r e n g e   _____

5.   w r l o g   _____

6.   w r o g n   _____

Macmillan/McGraw-Hill

6   Level 6/Unit 2
Consonant Blends: /gr/ *gr*

Extension: Have children list other words they know that begin with
/gr/ *gr* and make puzzles like those completed on this page. Children
can then solve each other's puzzles.

67

Short and Sweet

Read each story. Then put a line under the best summary.

1. Jay has a blue bird. Min has a black bird. Mary has two white birds.

   a. The birds like the children.
   b. All the children have birds.
   c. Birds make good pets.

2. We saw a black animal with white stripes. As we got closer we saw that it was starting to get angry. We left it alone!

   a. We saw a skunk.
   b. We got angry.
   c. We left the black animal.

3. Jake puts the towels and beach balls in the car. Then his dad packs the lunches. Jake can't wait to jump in the waves!

   a. Jake and his dad eat lunch.
   b. Jake's family goes to the beach.
   c. Jake throws beachballs.

4. I draw animals all the time. I also like to draw people. Sometimes I like to draw people while they work.

   a. I only draw people.
   b. I draw animals well.
   c. I like to draw.

5. We unpacked the boxes. We hung our pictures, and we moved our furniture. Now we are home!

   a. We moved the pictures.
   b. We bought new furniture.
   c. We moved into a new home.

Macmillan/McGraw-Hill

Extension: Ask children to summarize a story they know in a few sentences. Then ask others to guess the name of the story.

Level 6/Unit 2
Summarize

TIGER TRACKS

Think about "Nine-in-One, Grr! Grr!" Put an X by each sentence that tells about something that happened in this story.

_____ Tiger lived in the sky.

_____ The great god Shao knew everything.

_____ Tiger asks Shao how many cubs she will have.

_____ Tiger is sad after she talks to Shao.

_____ Tiger makes up a song to help her remember what Shao told her.

_____ Tiger forgets how to get home.

_____ Bird doesn't want Tiger to have nine cubs every year.

_____ Shao promises Bird he will change what he said to Tiger.

_____ Bird makes Tiger change her song.

_____ Tiger will have one cub every nine years.

Macmillan/McGraw-Hill

10 Level 6/Unit 2
Story Comprehension

Extension: Ask children how they would change the false statements on this page to make them true statements.

69

A Deer, Dear!

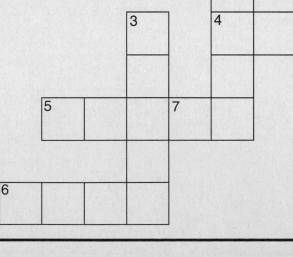

Look, d**ear**! It's a d**eer**.

First, read each clue. Then, unscramble the words in the box.
Finally, complete the puzzle.

| reed | erest | rae | raye | trae | reech |

Across

4. What you hear with

5. Hooray for our team!

6. When you cry, you shed
a _____.

Down

1. 12 months or 365 days

2. Animal who lives in the
woods

3. Make a car turn or go
straight

70 **Extension:** Have children write sentences using words with **eer** or **ear**.

Level 6/Unit 2
Variant Vowels and Phonograms /îr/
-eer, -ear   6

Macmillan/McGraw-Hill

TIGER TIME

TABLE OF CONTENTS

Chapter	Page
1. Where Tigers Live	2
2. The Body of a Tiger	14
3. Adult Tigers	20
4. Cubs	28
5. The Tiger's Hunt	34
6. History of Tigers	40

Use the Table of Contents above to answer the following questions. Circle the answer.

1. What is Chapter 3 called?

Adult Tigers   Cubs

The Tiger's Hunt

2. Which chapter begins on page 34?

Adult Tigers   Cubs

The Tiger's Hunt

3. On what page does the History of Tigers begin?

34   40   50

4. Which chapter tells about the tiger's home?

1   2   6

5. Which chapter tells about the tiger's feet?

2   3   4

6. Which chapter is the last one in the book?

Cubs   Adult Tigers

History of Tigers

Level 6/Unit 2
Information Resources: Table of Contents

Extension: Have children use books to find out about a tiger's home, life, and body.

71

Macmillan/McGraw-Hill

THE WEDNESDAY SURPRISE

Find the word that completes each sentence. Write the letter of the answer on the line.

_____ 1. Tony _____ the piano every day.

_____ 2. Grandma and Jess wanted to _____ reading the story.

_____ 3. "Surprise!" said Jess in a _____ voice.

_____ 4. Anna used her _____ to make pictures on the window.

_____ 5. Anna had a _____ idea for celebrating Tony's birthday.

_____ 6. Sasha _____ presents in colorful paper.

_____ 7. The dog ran _____ the party, trying to find the cake.

_____ 8. Grandma knew that Jess was _____ because she liked to read.

a. wonderful

b. finish

c. wrapped

d. smart

e. practiced

f. through

g. loud

h. breath

Extension: Have children write a list of things they do at a birthday party.

Name: _____ Date: _____

HOLD, HOME, HOSE

hold   home   hose

Use each word below to write about what is happening in the picture.

| sold | home | chose | rose | told |

_____

_____

_____

_____

_____

Macmillan/McGraw-Hill

5 Level 6/Unit 2
Long Vowels and Phonograms /ō/ -old, -ome, -ose

Extension: Have children brainstorm a list of words that rhyme with *hold*, *home*, and *hose* and then make up sentences using the words. Write the sentences on the chalkboard.

PRETTY AS A PICTURE

An idiom is a phrase that has a different meaning from what the words usually mean by themselves.

Idiom	Meaning
We were **up to our ears** in laundry.	We had a lot of clothes to wash.

Read each sentence and idiom. Then write the meaning of the idiom.

Idiom

Meaning

Michael couldn't go out to play. **It was raining cats and dogs.**

_____
_____

The children played and laughed. They were **having a ball.**

_____

Anna likes her new toy. She is **as happy as a clam.**

_____
_____

The dog ate the boy's homework. The boy got **bent out of shape.**

_____
_____

Extension: Ask children to give the meaning of these idioms: I was shaking in my boots, She almost bit my head off, Dad says our car is a lemon.

Level 6/Unit 2
Idioms

4

Macmillan/McGraw-Hill

PLAY BALL!

Read the story. Then answer each question. Use a complete sentence.

Billy stepped up to the plate. His knees were shaking, and he wished that he could just sit on the bench. He was only playing this game because his brother needed another player. The ball flew by him twice, and twice he swung at it. Then Billy just closed his eyes and swung one more time. CRACK! Billy's mouth dropped open as he watched the ball go over the fence.

1. What sport is Billy playing?

_____

2. How do you know this?

_____

_____

3. How does Billy feel about this game?

_____

_____

4. How do you think Billy feels at the end?

_____

_____

Macmillan/McGraw-Hill

Level 6/Unit 2
Make Inferences

Extension: Ask children to name the clues they found in the story to help them answer questions 3 and 4.

LET'S VISIT!

In the story "The Wednesday Surprise," Anna, Sam, and Grandma do the same things every Wednesday. Write the things they do between the time Grandma arrives and the time Grandma leaves.

Grandma arrives.

Anna and Grandma tell each other

_____

Ann shows Grandma her

_____

They always eat

_____

After dinner Anna and Grandma

_____

Sam walks Grandma to

_____

Grandma is at her home.

Extension: Have children work in groups of three and act out the parts of Anna, Grandma, and Sam. Have them use this story map as a guide to follow.

Level 6/Unit 2
Analyze Story Elements: Character, Plot

5

Macmillan/McGraw-Hill

A PRESENT FOR YOU

I bought a birthday **pr**esent for you.

Read each word. Then unscramble the letters to make a word
that rhymes. Write the word you make.

1. dress   s e r p s   _____

2. rinse   c r e p n i   _____

3. hint   n i p t r   _____

4. city   t y e r p t   _____

5. eyes   z i p e r   _____

6. cloud   r o d u p   _____

Macmillan/McGraw-Hill

PICTURE PREDICTIONS

Pretend each picture is from a story you are about to read. What do you think the story will be about? Underline the sentence.

1.

   a. Tom helps wash the car.

   b. Tom learns how to change a tire.

   c. Tom learns how to drive.

2.

   a. Baby birds eat worms.

   b. Baby birds build a nest.

   c. Baby birds learn to fly.

3.

   a. The family is going to the beach.

   b. The family is going shopping.

   c. The family is going to the library.

4.

   a. Lauren goes to school.

   b. Lauren scores a goal.

   c. Lauren stops the ball.

5.

   a. Chris does homework.

   b. Chris bakes a cake.

   c. Chris makes a wish.

Macmillan/McGraw-Hill

78

Extension: Ask children to give their reasons for the predictions they made for each exercise.

Level 6/Unit 2
Make, Confirm, or Revise Predictions

5

MAGIC CLUES

Read the story. Write the answer to each question. Use a complete sentence.

Jamie loves to do magic tricks. She wants to buy the magic kit in Mr. Britt's store, but she must wait until she has saved enough money from her weekly allowance. Every day she walks by the store to make sure the kit is in the window. Mr. Britt told her he would save one for her. Many weeks later, Jamie finally has enough money. When she gets to the store, the kit is gone from the window!

I. Do you think that the magic kit costs a little bit of money or a lot of money?

_____

2. What makes you think this?

_____

3. How do you think Jamie felt when the magic kit was gone?

_____

_____

4. Do you think Jamie got the magic kit? Why?

_____

_____

Macmillan/McGraw-Hill

Level 6/Unit 2
Draw Conclusions

Extension: Have children change some of the information in the story. Ask them how this would change the conclusions they first made about Jamie and the magic kit.

SURPRISE, SURPRISE!

Think about "The Wednesday Surprise." Finish each
sentence by underlining the answer.

1. Grandma takes care of Anna
   _____.

   a. every day

   b. only on Wednesdays

2. Anna's dad is a _____.

   a. truck driver

   b. pilot

3. Anna and Grandma want to
   surprise Dad because _____.

   a. it is his birthday

   b. he got a new job

4. Anna and Grandma have
   worked together to _____.

   a. teach Anna how to read

   b. teach Grandma
   how to read

5. Anna is nervous at the party
   because _____.

   a. she wants Grandma
   to read well.

   b. she wants to read well

6. Dad is crying at the end of
   the story because _____.

   a. he is sad that his
   surprise is over

   b. Grandma can read

80   **Extension:** Have children draw a picture of their favorite part of the
story. Then ask them to write a sentence about it.

Level 6/Unit 2
Story Comprehension   6

Macmillan/McGraw-Hill

I Ought to Have Caught the Ball!

ball   caught   bought

Write the word that rhymes with the underlined word in each sentence. Use the following words.

| fought | hall | taught | bought | wall |

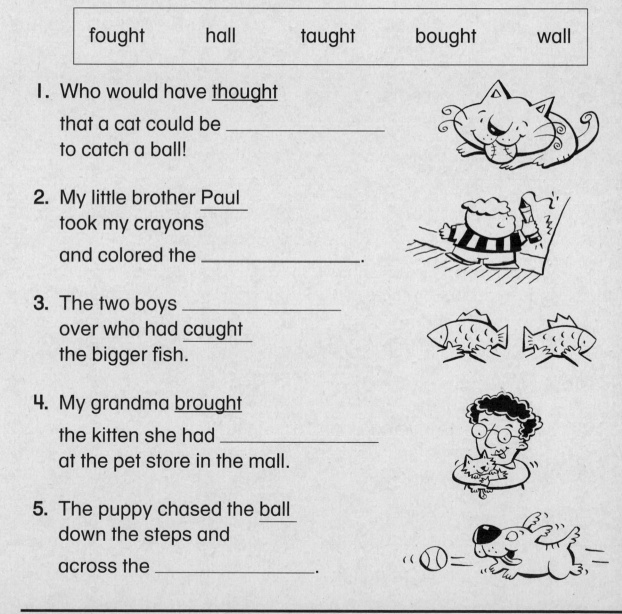

I. Who would have <u>thought</u>
that a cat could be _____
to catch a ball!

2. My little brother <u>Paul</u>
took my crayons

and colored the _____.

3. The two boys _____
over who had <u>caught</u>
the bigger fish.

4. My grandma <u>brought</u>

the kitten she had _____
at the pet store in the mall.

5. The puppy chased the <u>ball</u>
down the steps and

across the _____.

5

Level 6/Unit 2
**Variant Vowels and Phonograms /ô/
-all, -aught, -ought**

Extension: Have children brainstorm a list of words that rhyme with *ball* and *caught/bought* and then use the words to make their own rhymes.

81

Macmillan/McGraw-Hill

UNIT VOCABULARY REVIEW

Look at each group of words. Listen to your teacher say the words.
Underline the word that comes **first** in alphabetical order.

1. growled	2. sunlight	3. middle	4. wonderful
airplane	finish	Earth	beyond
lonely	busy	smart	happen
5. explained	6. kitchen	7. strong	8. important
loud	breath	forget	mother
straight	forest	answer	either

Look at each group of words. Listen to your teacher say the words.
Underline the word that comes **last** in alphabetical order.

9. beyond	10. practiced	11. finish	12. lonely
sunlight	explained	pretend	important
wrapped	grabbed	busy	through
13. quick	14. shining	15. kitchen	16. rushing
forget	airplane	safe	happen
Earth	wild	wonderful	loud

82 **Extension:** Have each child use a different word in a sentence.

Level 6/Unit 2
Unit Vocabulary Review 16

Macmillan/McGraw-Hill

THE MYSTERIOUS TADPOLE

An **analogy** compares words or things.

| short is to tall | **short : tall** |

as

| little is to big | **little : big** |

These words are the opposite of each other.

Work in pairs. Read the incomplete analogies. Circle the word that completes the analogy.

1. people: apartment
birds: _____

   nest   hole   never

2. bottom: top
morning: _____

   nothing   night   open

3. house: build
tunnel: _____

   dig   dance   goat

4. often: never
early: _____

   lost   gate   late

5. planet: Earth
state: _____

   lonely   sleep   Texas

6. chest: treasure
envelope: _____

   better   letter   boys

7. nature: flower
man-made: _____

   building   carry   shell

8. grow to be: become
stop: _____

   carry   smart   end

Macmillan/McGraw-Hill

8

Level 6/Unit 3
Selection Vocabulary

Extension: Have children work in pairs and use other words from "The Mysterious Tadpole" to make analogies.

83

MORE MEANINGS

The underlined words in the sentences have more than one meaning. Read each sentence. Fill in the circle next to the meaning of the underlined word.

1. Mother washes the dishes in the <u>sink</u>.

   ⓐ to go to the bottom

   ⓑ a place to put water

2. The boat will <u>sink</u> to the bottom of the pool.

   ⓐ to go to the bottom

   ⓑ a place to put water

3. The <u>building</u> is ten stories high.

   ⓐ making something

   ⓑ something with a roof and walls

4. They are <u>building</u> a house out of blocks.

   ⓐ making something

   ⓑ something with a roof and walls

5. <u>Raise</u> your hand before speaking in class.

   ⓐ to lift higher

   ⓑ to collect money for a purpose

6. They will <u>raise</u> money for a new school bus.

   ⓐ to lift higher

   ⓑ to collect money for a purpose

Macmillan/McGraw-Hill

Extension: Have children brainstorm other multiple-meaning words and use them in sentences.

Level 6/Unit 3
CONTEXT CLUES: Multiple-Meaning Words

 6

BELIEVE IT OR NOT!

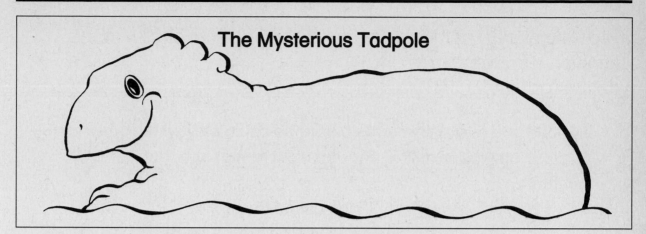

The Mysterious Tadpole

Think about "The Mysterious Tadpole." Write two things from the story that could really happen. Then write two things from the story that are make-believe.

Real Things	**Make-Believe Things**
Louis's uncle lives in Scotland.	The tadpole grows too big for the house.

Extension: Ask children to tell something that their pet or an animal they know can really do. Then have them tell something about the animal that could not happen in real life.

Macmillan/McGraw-Hill

Barn Buddies

Read the story. Then circle the word or words that best complete each sentence.

Joe had to do his chores before he could play with his friends. His last job was to milk Buffy. Joe went to the barn, but Buffy was not there.

"Have you seen Buffy?" Joe asked his brother.

"Not since yesterday when I milked her," said Bill.

Bill and Joe looked at the latch on Buffy's stall. It was broken.

"Oh no!" said Joe. "She got out! Look! She is in the garden!"

"Let's go!" said Bill.

1. Buffy is a _____ .   horse   cow

2. Joe's brother's   Bill   Buffy
   name is _____ .

3. Buffy lives in the   barn   house
   _____ .

4. Buffy got out of   Bill forgot to   the latch was broken
   her stall because   milk her
   _____ .

5. Joe and Bill go to   get Buffy   play with friends
   _____ .

Extension: Ask children to create an ending to this story based on their conclusions.

Level 6/Unit 3
Draw Conclusions

5

Macmillan/McGraw-Hill

/ô/-ALL, -AUGHT, OR -OUGHT?

Who **c**augh**t** the b**all**?   She **b**ough**t** a toy.

Write the words to finish the puzzle. Use the words in the box.

| fall | caught | thought | tall | taught | bought | call | ball |

Across

1. not short, but _____

3. round as a _____

4. say in a loud voice

5. helped to learn

6. not sold, but _____

Down

1. an idea

2. between summer and winter

4. took and held

Level 6/Unit 3
Variant Vowels and Phonograms /ô/
-all, -aught, -ought

Extensions: Have children think of other words that end in **all**, **aught**, and **ought** and use the words to make their own crossword puzzles.

87

Macmillan/McGraw-Hill

SMOKE SMELLS!

Do you **sm**ell **sm**oke?

Finish the labels for each chart. Use these words.

| smooth | smell | small | smile |

Things that make you _____	Things that are _____
• a joke	• ants
• a funny book	• raisins
• a hug from your mom and dad	• babies
Things that are _____	Things that _____ good
• glass	• baking bread
• marbles	• roses
• a baby's skin	• turkey dinner

Extension: Write other **sm** words on index cards, shuffle them, and place the cards face down. As children draw several cards, have them say the words and then arrange the words in alphabetical order.

88

Level 6/Unit 3
Consonant Blends /sm/ *sm*

4

Macmillan/McGraw-Hill

WHAT DO THEY THINK?

Think about "The Mysterious Tadpole." Write the name of
each person in the story under each picture. Then tell what
each person thinks about Alphonse.

1. _____

_____   _____

_____

2. _____

_____   _____

3. _____

_____   _____

4. _____

_____   _____

5. _____

_____   _____

Level 6/Unit 3
**ANALYZE STORY ELEMENTS: Character,
Plot, Setting**

Extension: Ask children to tell where they might be if they happened to
see each of these people. For example, they might be in Scotland if
they saw Uncle McAllister.

89

Macmillan/McGraw-Hill

THAT ABOUT SUMS IT UP

Tell about "The Mysterious Tadpole." Fill in the chart below.

1. Important people and animals in the story: _____

_____

2. Problem: _____

_____

_____

_____

3. What happens: _____

_____

_____

_____

4. Outcome: _____

_____

5. Ending: _____

_____

Extension: Have children practice summarizing by telling what they did last evening.

Level 6/Unit 3
Summarize

5

Macmillan/McGraw-Hill

ADDING ON

You can add a prefix, or a letter or letters, to the beginning of some words. In **unhappy**, **disagree**, and **reopen**, **un**, **dis**, and **re** are prefixes. Knowing what a prefix means can help you to figure out what a word means.

prefix	meaning
un	not, opposite of
dis	not, opposite of
re	again

Unhappy means "not happy." **Disagree** means "the opposite of agree." **Reopen** means "open again."

Read the paragraph. Underline the words with the prefixes **un**, **dis**, and **re**. List the words, circle the prefixes, and write the meaning of each word.

My brother is learning to do some magic tricks. Some of the tricks are unbelievable. The other day he made our gerbil disappear. With a wave of his wand, he made it reappear. Then he put a coin in my scarf and folded it. When he unfolded it, the coin was gone! I think it's unfair that he won't show me how to do the tricks.

_____

_____

_____

10

Level 6/Unit 3
STRUCTURAL CLUES: Prefixes and Suffixes

Extension: Have children begin a chart to record words they find that begin with prefixes **dis-**, **un-**, and **re-**.

91

Macmillan/McGraw-Hill

BIRTHDAY SURPRISE

Think about "The Mysterious Tadpole." Answer each question. Write complete sentences.

1. What kind of gift does Louis always get from his uncle?

_____

_____

2. What is so mysterious about the tadpole?

_____

_____

3. Why is it important for Louis to find a swimming pool for Alphonse?

_____

_____

_____

4. How do you think Louis's parents feel when they see the second present Uncle McAllister has sent Louis?

_____

_____

_____

Extension: Ask children to tell what they would have done if Alphonse was their pet and he grew too large for their homes.

Macmillan/McGraw-Hill

COOL SCHOOL

sch**ool**   m**oon**

Circle the word that answers the riddle. Then write the word.

1. This is what thread comes wrapped around.

_____

spoon   spool   stool

2. This is something you need to eat soup.

_____

soon   pool   spoon

3. This is something you can sit on.

_____

stool   stove   spoon

4. This is something you can use to fix things.

_____

school   tool   spoon

5. This pops if you blow it up too much.

_____

cartoon   spool   balloon

6. This animal looks like it is wearing a mask.

_____

raccoon   afternoon   cartoon

6

Level 6/Unit 3
Variant Vowels and Phonograms /ü/
-ool, -oon

Extension: Have children brainstorm other words that end like **school** and **moon** and then make up their own riddles.

93

Macmillan/McGraw-Hill

NOVEMBER NEWS

NOVEMBER NEWS						
SUN	MON	TUE	WED	THU	FRI	SAT
		1	2	3 New Moon	4	5
6	7	8	9	10	11 Veterans' Day	12
13	14	15 Pam's Party	16	17	18	19
20	21 Order Turkey	22	23 Pick up Turkey	24 Thanksgiving	25 No School	26
27	28	29	30			

Use this calendar to finish each sentence.

1. November has _____ days.

    3   20   30

2. Pam's party is the _____ .

    5th   15th   25th

3. Order the turkey _____ days before Thanksgiving.

    3   4   5

4. There will be no school on November _____ .

    25th   28th   29th

Extension: Have children create a calendar for the month in which their birthday falls. Have them highlight their birthday and other important days in that month.

94

Level 6/Unit 3
Reference Sources: Calendar

4

Macmillan/McGraw-Hill

MORE MEANINGS

Read the sentences. Write the meaning of the word in **bold print** on the line.

1. The Navajo used strong, colorful **yarn** to weave rugs.

_____

2. It is **easier** to say a short name than a long name.

_____

3. The **large** comb was bigger than her hands.

_____

4. The red **dye** colored the yarn.

_____

5. She grabbed the yarn and **pulled** it toward her.

_____

6. She pulls and twists the fiber to **spin** wool into yarn.

_____

7. **Twigs** from a tree can stick to an animal's fur.

_____

8. The **wool** on some goats is called mohair.

_____

Macmillan/McGraw-Hill

Level 6/Unit 3
Selection Vocabulary

Extension: Have children use at least three boldfaced words to describe a picture they draw.

95

A SPECIAL SPOT

This is my **sp**ecial **sp**ot.

Read each word. Then unscramble the letters to make a word that rhymes. Write the word you make on the line.

1. rider   d r i p e s   _____

2. June   p o n s o   _____

3. thin   p i n s   _____

4. trace   c a p e s   _____

5. chill   l i p s l   _____

6. bend   d e s n p   _____

Macmillan/McGraw-Hill

Extension: Have children make a list of other words that begin with *sp* and then create their own scrambled word puzzles.

Level 6/Unit 3
Consonant Blends /sp/ *sp*   6

Name: _____   Date: _____

CLUE CLENCHING

To figure out the meaning of words you don't know, you can use other words you know. This is using **context clues.**

yucca	lather	burrs
fibers	dyeing	loom

Read the pages from "The Goat in the Rug" under each word. Then use context clues from the story to match each word with its meaning. Write the letter of the answer on the line.

a. yucca
Page 274

b. lather
Page 274

c. burrs
Page 275

d. fibers
Page 275

e. dyeing
Page 281

f. loom
Page 284

1. types of threads _____

2. making something a new color _____

3. sticky parts of a plant _____

4. foam made when soap is mixed with water _____

5. a frame used for weaving yarn into cloth _____

6. a plant that grows in the desert _____

Macmillan/McGraw-Hill

Name: _____ Date: _____

The Goat in the Rug
PHONICS: Variant Vowels and Phonograms
/är/ -ark, -ar

A Bright Star on a Dark Night

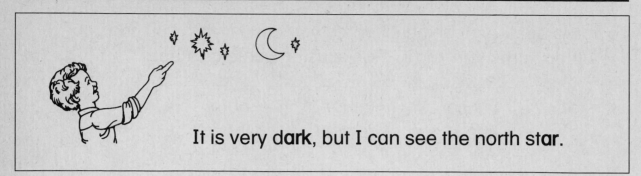

It is very d**ark**, but I can see the north st**ar**.

Write the word that tells about the picture. Use the words in the box.

bark	star	park	jar	shark

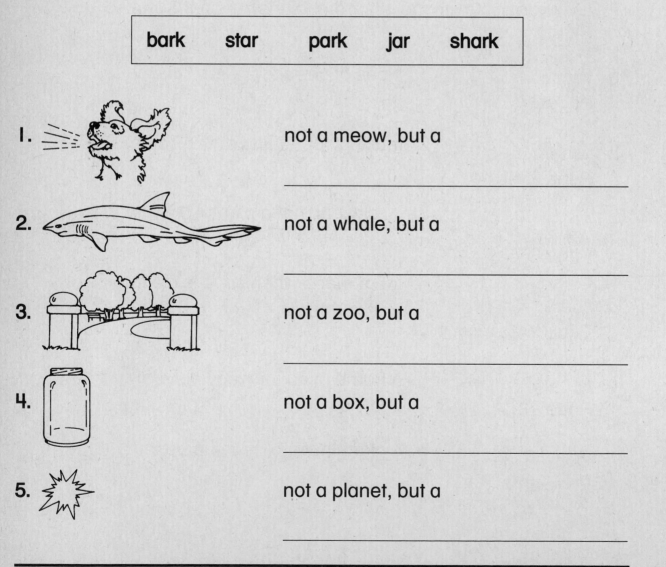

1. not a meow, but a

   _____

2. not a whale, but a

   _____

3. not a zoo, but a

   _____

4. not a box, but a

   _____

5. not a planet, but a

   _____

Extension: Encourage children to look for and list words with **-ark** and **-ar** that they find in story books and magazines, and then make up their own sentences using the words.

Level 6/Unit 3
Variant Vowels and Phonograms /är/ -ark, -ar

5

PET FACTS

Pretend your dad is giving you a pet as a surprise. You are trying to guess what kind of pet it is. Read each fact.
Circle YES if it would help you guess what is inside the box. Circle NO if the information is not important.

1. The animal's box is very big.   yes   no

2. The box is brown.   yes   no

3. You see a leash coming out of the box.   yes   no

4. You have always wanted a pet.   yes   no

5. The food dish is large and heavy.   yes   no

6. The food dish is blue.   yes   no

7. A tail is sticking out of the box.   yes   no

8. You hear the pet make a sound.   yes   no

9. The pet toy is in the shape of a bone.   yes   no

10. There is only one toy.   yes   no

Macmillan/McGraw-Hill

10 Level 6/Unit 3
Important and Unimportant Information

Extension: Ask children to draw a picture of the surprise pet and then write a sentence about it.

99

LET'S GET MOVING

Read the story and the sentences below it. Write 1, 2, 3, 4, or 5 next to each sentence to show the order of the story events.

Drew watched as the big moving van pulled up to his house. He wondered how the movers would get everything packed into the van. First they wrapped all the dishes and packed them into boxes. Then they packed clothes and other things into more boxes.

The next day the movers carried all the furniture to the van. Then they placed all the boxes around the furniture. Drew waved good-bye to the movers as they backed the van out of his driveway.

_____ The boxes are placed around the furniture.

_____ The furniture is placed in the van.

_____ Drew sees the moving van come to his house.

_____ Drew waves good-bye to the movers.

_____ The movers pack boxes.

Macmillan/McGraw-Hill

100 **Extension:** Have children work in pairs and tell each other the steps involved in tying their shoes or putting on a jacket.

Level 6/Unit 3
ORGANIZE INFORMATION: Steps in a Process

RUG REMINDERS

Reread "The Goat in the Rug." Complete the sentences to tell the steps Glenmae followed to make her rug.

How to Make a Rug

1. First, you clip _____.

   _____

2. Wash the wool until it is _____.

   _____

3. Use carding combs to _____.

   _____

4. Spin the wool to _____.

   _____

5. Dip the wool in _____.

   _____

6. Weave a design using a _____.

   _____

Macmillan/McGraw-Hill

GOAT NOTES

Think about "The Goat in the Rug." Read the sentences below that tell what happened. Then write why each thing happened.

What happened?   **Why did it happen?**

Glenmae clipped wool
from Geraldine.   _____

                                      _____

Glenmae chopped roots
from a yucca tree.   _____

                                      _____

Glenmae walked miles to
a store.   _____

                                      _____

Glenmae dipped white
wool into a big pot.   _____

                                      _____

Glenmae set up a loom.   _____

                                      _____

Geraldine's wool has
grown long again.   _____

                                      _____

Extension: Ask children to act out something that Glenmae does in the story. Ask others to tell what is happening.

Level 6/Unit 3
Story Comprehension

Macmillan/McGraw-Hill

The Goat in the Rug
PHONICS: VARIANT VOWELS AND PHONOGRAMS
/âr/ -air, -are

Name: _____   Date: _____

HAIR CARE

Brushing is one way to **care** for your **hair**

Write the word that names the picture.

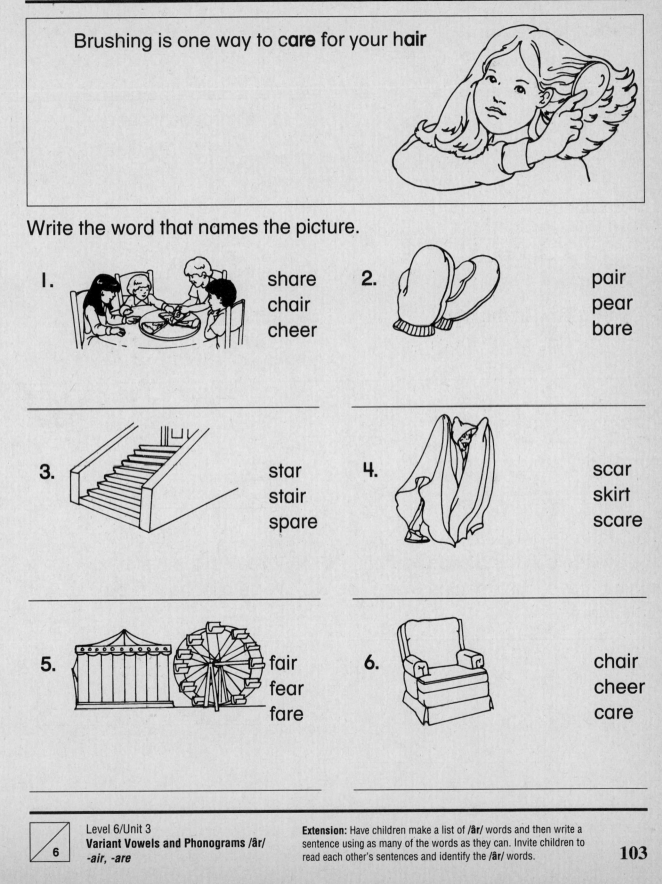

1. share
    chair
    cheer

2. pair
    pear
    bare

3. star
    stair
    spare

4. scar
    skirt
    scare

5. fair
    fear
    fare

6. chair
    cheer
    care

Extension: Have children make a list of /âr/ words and then write a sentence using as many of the words as they can. Invite children to read each other's sentences and identify the /âr/ words.

DOTS AND DOORS

Follow the directions.

1. Put dots on the rock.
Put stripes on the rock.

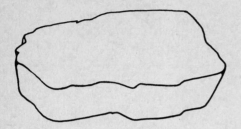

2. Put wool on the goat. Put
a bell around its neck.

3. Put food in the pot.
Put clothes on the
clothesline.

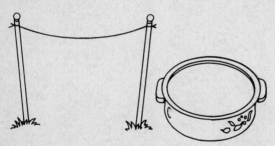

4. Put a door on the house.
Put leaves on the flower.

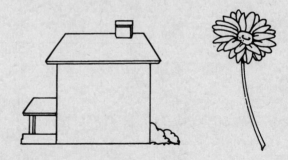

5. Write **b** in the box on the left.
Write **e** in the box on the
right.

6. Write **r** in the first box.
Write **g** in the last box.

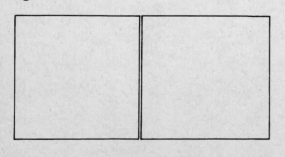

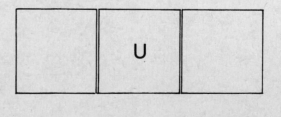

Extension: Have children draw something with missing parts. Have
them write directions for placing the parts on the object.

Level 6/Unit 3
Study Skills: Follow Directions

Macmillan/McGraw-Hill

HENRY'S WRONG TURN

ocean	bridge	harbor	whale
noticed	signaled	courses	

Read the sentences. Write a word from the box that means almost the same thing as the word or words in **bold print**.

1. The ship sailed into the **safe place near the shore.** _____

2. The movie is about a **large animal that lives in the ocean.** _____

3. The ship can take different **ways to get from here to there.** _____

4. The bus went over the **path or road built across water.** _____

5. My dog ran to me when I **showed what to do without words.** _____

6. Which **large body of salt water** is this? _____

7. We **saw** a beautiful butterfly flying in the garden. _____

7 Level 6/Unit 3
Selection Vocabulary

Extension: Have children rewrite the sentences with the words they used for answers.

105

Macmillan/McGraw-Hill

PICK A GROUP

Look at the picture. Underline the group to which the picture could belong.

Things You Turn On
Things You Throw
Animals
Trees

Colorful Things
Sharp Things
Things That Help You Write
Musical Instruments

Large Plants
Purple Things
Things With Spots
Fish

Places
Sad Things
Food
Things With Buttons

Fast Things
Furry Animals
Slow Things
Pink Things

Extension: Ask children to name as many objects in each underlined
category as they can. Use their responses to make a list for each
category.

106

Level 6/Unit 3
ORGANIZE INFORMATION: Categories

5

Macmillan/McGraw-Hill

SPACE JOURNEY

Read the story. Use word clues to help you figure out the meanings of the underlined words. Then draw a line to match each underlined word with its meaning.

When I look at the sky through my <u>telescope</u> I wonder what space is like. Some nights I see a <u>comet</u> falling through the sky. It looks like a long-haired star. Someday I hope to be an <u>astronaut</u> and to travel in space. I might visit a planet like <u>Jupiter</u>. Maybe I will find a new <u>galaxy</u> of stars like the Milky Way.

telescope   the largest known planet

comet   a person trained to make rocket
                                             flights in space

astronaut   an instrument that makes far-off
                                             objects seem closer

Jupiter   a very large group of stars

galaxy   a bright ball of gas that looks like
                                             it has a tail

Macmillan/McGraw-Hill

5 Level 6/Unit 3
   CONTEXT CLUES: Unfamiliar Words

Extension: Ask children to draw a space picture that shows some of the things named on this page. Encourage children to write about their pictures.

Wrong Way Whale

In the story "Henry's Wrong Turn," Henry swims past many things. Write what Henry does between the time he enters New York Harbor and the time he leaves it.

Henry swims into New York Harbor.

Henry swims _____

Henry swims _____

Henry swims _____

Henry swims _____

Henry swims _____

Henry swims _____

Henry swims out to sea.

Extension: Act out the sequence of the story by asking one child to be Henry and the other children to be tourists who see Henry at each spot he swims past.

Level 6/Unit 3
ORGANIZE INFORMATION: Sequence of Events

Macmillan/McGraw-Hill

SPRINKLE THE SPROUTS

I **spr**inkle the growing **spr**outs each day.

Write the word that rhymes with the underlined words in each sentence. Use the following words.

| spring spread spray sprout |

1.

Said the pumpkin to a seed,
"Do not <u>pout</u>.
I have no <u>doubt</u>

one day you'll _____."

2.

"I'm hungry!" <u>said</u> <u>Fred</u> .

"What can I _____
on my <u>bread</u>?"

3.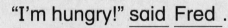

"April Showers" is a song we <u>sing</u>

to welcome the coming of _____.

4.

We like to <u>play</u>

under the cool _____
of our garden hose
on a hot summer day.

Macmillan/McGraw-Hill

Extension: Have children brainstorm a list of words that begin with **spr** and then use the words to create their own rhymes.

STEER CLEAR

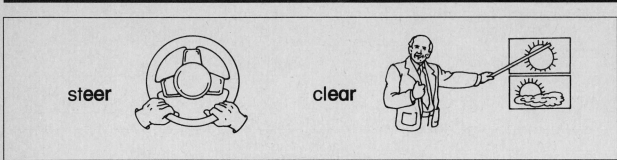

steer   clear

Use the words from the box to complete the sentences.

| deer   steer   disappear   cheer   ear |

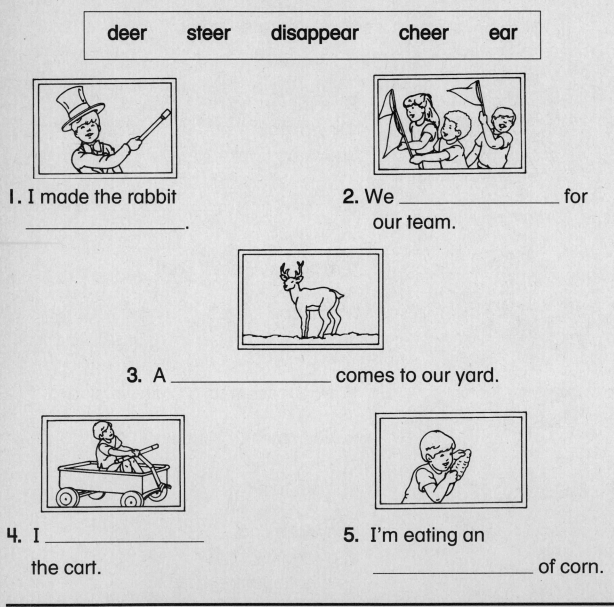

1. I made the rabbit _____.

2. We _____ for our team.

3. A _____ comes to our yard.

4. I _____ the cart.

5. I'm eating an _____ of corn.

Extension: Have children brainstorm a list of words that rhymes with **steer** and **clear**. Write the words on the chalkboard. Have children take turns reading the words and using them in sentences.

Level 6/Unit 3
Variant Vowels and Phonograms /îr/-*ear*, -*eer*

5

Macmillan/McGraw-Hill

HOME SWEET HOME

The reason why something happens is the **cause**. What happens is the **effect.**

Think about "Henry's Wrong Turn." Read the sentences below that tell what happened. Then write why each thing happened.

What happened?

Why did it happen?

The tugboat captain signaled to all the other boats.

_____
_____

Everyone was on the lookout for Henry.

_____
_____

The ferries veered off their courses.

_____
_____

The Coast Guard boat stayed close to Henry.

_____
_____

4 Level 6/Unit 3
ORGANIZE INFORMATION: Cause and Effect

Extension: Ask children to make up something that might have happened to Henry. Then ask them to tell why it happened. Have children identify the cause and the effect.

111

Macmillan/McGraw-Hill

WHALE OF A TALE

Think about "Henry's Wrong Turn." Underline the best answer to complete each sentence.

1. Usually a whale like Henry would swim out to _____.

   a. sea

   b. New York Harbor

2. In New York Harbor there is nothing for Henry to _____.

   a. do

   b. eat

3. The tugboat captain signaled other boats to _____.

   a. watch out for Henry

   b. catch Henry

4. Compared to the Queen Elizabeth 2, Henry was _____.

   a. small

   b. large

5. The Coast Guard wanted to help Henry _____.

   a. find a home in the harbor

   b. get back out to sea

6. Henry was in danger of _____.

   a. getting lost at sea

   b. getting hit by boats

7. People on the *Intrepid* cheered because Henry _____.

   a. made loud noises

   b. sent up a spray of water

8. Everyone was excited about Henry because _____.

   a. no one could remember seeing a whale in the harbor

   b. Henry does tricks

Macmillan/McGraw-Hill

Extension: Ask children to pretend they are Henry and to describe what they are seeing as they swim around New York Harbor.

Level 6/Unit 3
Story Comprehension

A Whale of a "Tail"

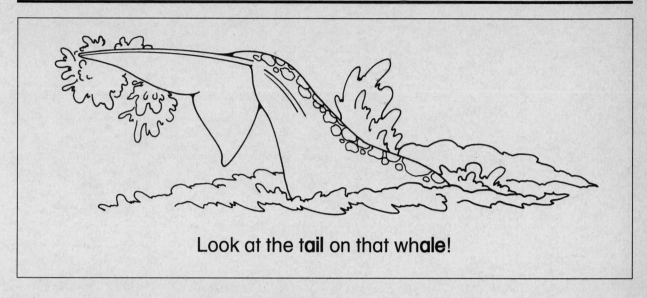

Look at the **t**a**il** on that wh**ale**!

Write the word that names the picture.

1. 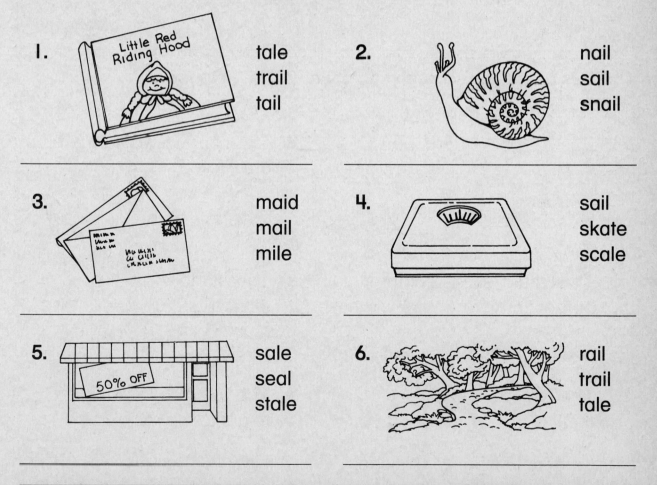 tale
   trail
   tail

2. nail
    sail
    snail

3. maid
    mail
    mile

4. sail
    skate
    scale

5. sale
    seal
    stale

6. rail
    trail
    tale

6

Level 6/Unit 3
Long Vowels and Phonograms /ā/-ale, -ail

Extension: Have pairs of children list at least ten words that rhyme with **whale** and **tail**. Children can then use index cards to make two sets of word cards to play matching games.

113

Macmillan/McGraw-Hill

FIND THE FERRY

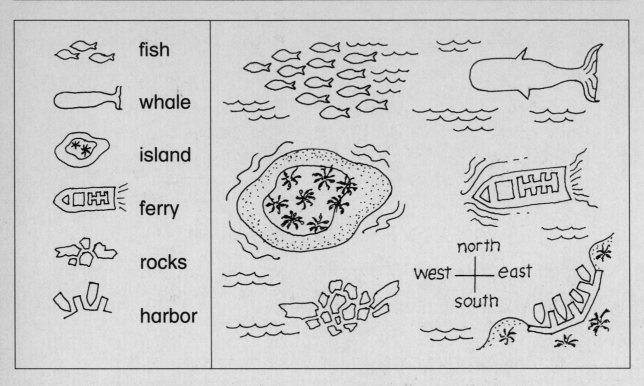

Use this map to finish each sentence. Circle the answer.

1. _____ shows where there are fish.

2. _____ shows where there are rocks.

3. The whale is _____ of the harbor.

   south   north   east

4. The island is _____ of the ferry.

   west   east   south

5. The ferry is east of the _____.

   harbor   whale   island

6. The fish must swim _____ to get to the rocks.

   west   south   north

114 **Extension:** Have children use symbols to make a map of the school.

Level 6/Unit 3
Graphic Aids: Maps

Macmillan/McGraw-Hill

SWIMMY

corner	shell	suddenly	rainbow
escaped	scared	hidden	giant

Read the story. Choose a word from the box to complete each sentence. Write the word in the sentence. Then reread the story to check your answers.

Last summer, my family spent a week at the seashore.

On the first afternoon, we walked along the beach. Out of

the _____ of my eye I saw something

_____ in the sand. I pulled it out gently.

It was a _____ _____. It shone with

_____ colors. I put it in my beach bag. After

we walked and played for two hours, the sky turned gray. It started

to rain _____. We _____ the

downpour by finding shelter. I was a little _____

when it started to thunder, but Mom said not to worry because we

were in a safe place. Soon the rain stopped and the sun came out.

It turned out to be a great day after all!

Macmillan/McGraw-Hill

 Level 6/Unit 3
Selection Vocabulary

Extension: Have children put the words in the box in alphabetical order.

115

You Should Have Been There!

Pretend that you are Swimmy. You are telling your fish friends what you have seen in the deep, wet world. Write about four things that you have seen. Then write about what each of these things looked like.

Dear Friends,

As I swam in the deep wet world, I saw many things. I saw a _____ that reminded me of a _____ . I saw a _____ that looked like _____. Then I saw _____ that moved like _____ . I also saw _____ who looked like _____.

Now let's go SEE more things!

116

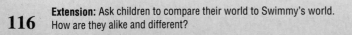
Extension: Ask children to compare their world to Swimmy's world. How are they alike and different?

Level 6/Unit 3
ANALYZE STORY ELEMENTS: Setting

8

Macmillan/McGraw-Hill

LET'S GO SWIMMING!

Swimming is so much fun!

Look at the clues. Write the words to finish the puzzle. Use these words.

| sweater | swimmer | swing | sweet | sweep |

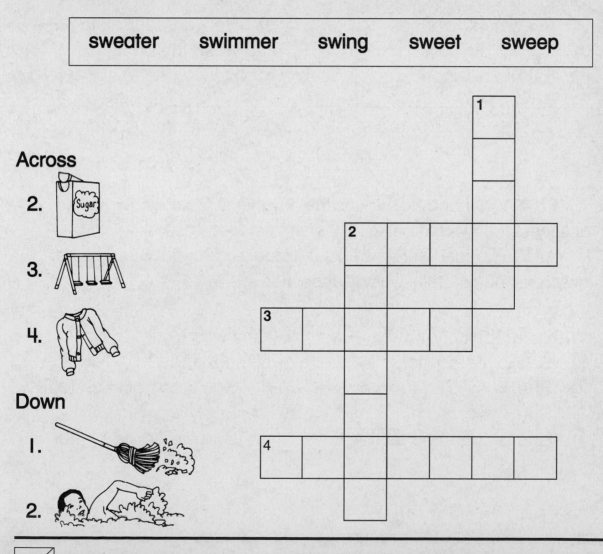

Across

2.

3.

4.

Down

1.

2.

Extension: Have children brainstorm a list of words that begin with **sw** and then use the words to create their own puzzles.

117

Macmillan/McGraw-Hill

Find Out Why

Read each story and the questions. Fill in the circle next to the answer to each question.

Jake wanted to help his dad. He mowed the lawn. Then he washed his dad's car and shined his shoes.

When his dad came home and saw what Jake had done, he took Jake out for a special treat.

1. Why did Jake do all of those jobs?
   ⓐ to earn allowance
   ⓑ to help his dad
   ⓒ to help his mom

2. Why did Jake's dad take Jake out when he got home?
   ⓐ He wanted to help Jake wash the car.
   ⓑ He wanted to show off his shiny shoes.
   ⓒ He wanted to thank Jake.

Emily was happy. This was the day they were changing seats at school. She would get to sit by her best friend, Sue.

As Emily found her new spot, she looked around. Sue was not at school today. Emily was disappointed.

3. Why was Emily happy?
   ⓐ She loves school.
   ⓑ She was going to sit by Sue.
   ⓒ She is changing clothes.

4. Why was Emily disappointed?
   ⓐ Sue was not at school.
   ⓑ Emily was sick.
   ⓒ Sue did not sit by her.

Macmillan/McGraw-Hill

118 **Extension:** Ask children to make up a sentence about each story that uses the word **because**.

Level 6/Unit 3
ORGANIZE INFORMATION: Cause and Effect

PARTY PROBLEMS

Read the story. Then circle the word or words that best complete each sentence.

Jan makes a wish and blows out the candles on her cake. Now it is time to break the colorful paper piñata. Everyone knows that when the piñata breaks open, treats will fall to the floor.

First, Jan is blindfolded. She knows she has to swing the stick high to reach the piñata. On her first two swings she breaks the piñata's snout and its curly tail.

Now it is Bill's turn. Jan hands the blindfold to Bill. Whack! The children all run when they see the piñata break open.

1. Jan is at a _____.

birthday party

dance

2. The piñata is _____.

hanging from the ceiling

on a table

3. The piñata is shaped like a _____.

tiger

pig

4. Jan _____.

breaks open the piñata

does not break open the piñata

5. The piñata is broken open by _____.

Bill

Jan

6. The children are running to get the _____.

treats

stick

Level 6/Unit 3
Draw Conclusions

Extension: Ask children to name specific clues that helped them reach their conclusions.

119

Macmillan/McGraw-Hill

School at Noon

We got out of sch**ool** at n**oon** today.

Read each word. Then unscramble the letters to make a word that rhymes. Write the word you make.

1.	school	l o t s o	_____
2.	soon	p o n s o	_____
3.	fool	l o t o	_____
4.	balloon	c a r c o n o	_____
5.	drool	p o l o s	_____
6.	cool	c h o s o l	_____

120 **Extension:** Have children write a sentence for each word they wrote.

Level 6/Unit 3
Variant Vowels and Phonograms /ü/
-*ool*, -*oom*

Macmillan/McGraw-Hill

SWIMMING ALONG

Think about "Swimmy." Read these paragraphs from "Swimmy."

"Let's go and swim and play and SEE things!" he said happily.
"We can't," said the little red fish. "The big fish will eat us all."
"But you can't just lie there," said Swimmy. "We must THINK of something."

Write a complete sentence to answer each question.

1. What had Swimmy done right before this part of the story?

_____

_____

2. What did Swimmy do right after this part of the story?

_____

_____

3. What is important about this part of the story?

_____

_____

4. How do you think the little fish would describe Swimmy?

_____

_____

4 Level 6/Unit 3
Story Comprehension

Extension: Ask children to name things that Swimmy and the fish will see as they travel the deep, wet world.

121

Macmillan/McGraw-Hill

SOLVING RIDDLES

First p**eel** the banana.   Then f**eed** it to the monkey.

Circle the word that answers the riddle. Then write the word.

1. This looks like a snake and swims in the sea.

_____

seal   eel   eagle

2. This is what you don't want to grow in your garden.

_____

wheel   wide   weed

3. This is a round ring with spokes.

_____

wheel   weed   steel

4. This will grow when you plant it in the soil.

_____

need   seal   seed

5. This is a strong, hard metal.

_____

steep   seal   steel

6. This is the back of your foot.

_____

heel   peel   heal

122

Extension: Have children brainstorm other words that end like **peel** and **feed** and then make up their own riddles.

Level 6/Unit 3
Variant Vowels and Phonograms /ē/
-eel, -eed   6

Macmillan/McGraw-Hill

UNIT VOCABULARY REVIEW

Look at the words in each group. Underline the word your teacher says.

1. worry whale wool	2. ribbon rainbow raining	3. did dye day	4. over oven often
5. plant planet pulled	6. trust twigs treasure	7. build bridge bottom	8. courses corn corner
9. open ocean over	10. giant gain gate	11. enter escaped scale	12. native nature noticed
13. apple apartment always	14. land large longer	15. shell spin spit	16. east easy easier
17. yarn year yard	18. suddenly scared signaled	19. before between become	20. harbor high hidden

Macmillan/McGraw-Hill

20   Level 6/Unit 3
Unit Review Vocabulary

Extension: Have children orally give clues for the vocabulary words, and have other children tell the words they have described.

123

DEAR DADDY...

bought	ship	except	beach
listen	buy	huge	hope

Read the story. Choose a word from the box to complete each sentence. Write the word in the sentence. Then reread the story to check your answers.

Yesterday I _____ a new bathing suit to take

with me to the _____ . My family and I cannot

wait to go swimming in the cool ocean water. Everyone

_____ my little brother is a good swimmer.

I like to _____ to the sound of the

_____ waves as they crash onto the shore.

Sometimes I see a _____ far off in the distance.

Someday I _____ to travel around the world.

Maybe I will even be able to _____ my own boat!

124

Extension: Have children draw something that is huge and write a sentence about it.

Level 7/Unit 1
Selection Vocabulary

8

SHOW ME A RIDDLE

The answer to each riddle starts with **sh**. The picture gives a clue. Write the word next to the riddle.

1. It is something you put on each foot. _____

2. It can be found on a beach. _____

3. It sails on the sea. _____

4. It sometimes has buttons. _____

5. They may be in a flock. _____

5 | Level 7/Unit 1
Consonant Digraphs /sh/*sh*

Extension: Have children make up a sentence using each word they wrote.

125

Macmillan/McGraw-Hill

AWAY FOR A DAY

The **wait**ress brought a t**ray** with a huge birth**day** cake.

Write the word from the box that has the opposite meaning of the underlined word.

wait	play	yesterday	away	today

1. not to <u>work</u>, but to _____

2. not <u>tonight</u>, but _____

3. not <u>go on</u>, but _____

4. not <u>near</u>, but far _____

5. not <u>tomorrow</u>, but _____

126 **Extension:** Have children say words that rhyme with **day**.

Level 7/Unit 1
Long Vowels and Phonograms
/ā/ -ay, -ait

5

Macmillan/McGraw-Hill

A WEATHER MAP

Use the map of England to answer the questions. Write the answers on the lines.

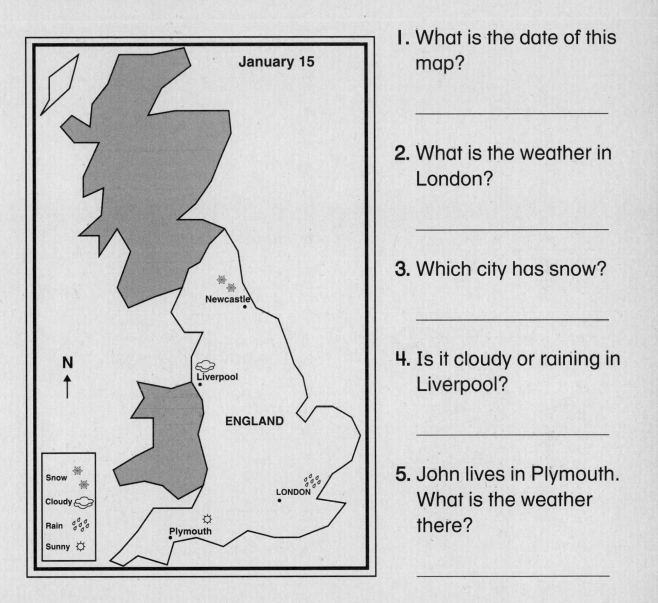

January 15

Newcastle

Liverpool

ENGLAND

N

LONDON

Plymouth

Snow
Cloudy
Rain
Sunny

1. What is the date of this map?

_____

2. What is the weather in London?

_____

3. Which city has snow?

_____

4. Is it cloudy or raining in Liverpool?

_____

5. John lives in Plymouth. What is the weather there?

_____

Level 7/Unit 1
GRAPHIC AIDS: Maps

Extension: Display a map of the U.S. on a bulletin board. Have children make cut-out symbols for weather to pin to it daily, using the newspaper weather map as a guide.

Macmillan/McGraw-Hill

PICTURE THIS

Look at each picture. Circle the letter next to the sentence that tells about the picture.

1.

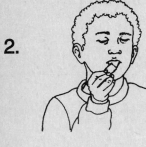

a. The boy is writing a letter.

b. The boy is reading a book.

2.

a. He licks the envelope.

b. He licks the stamp.

3.

a. The boy mails the letter.

b. The boy opens the letter.

4.

a. The mail has arrived.

b. Pizza is delivered.

5.

a. Grandpa likes old movies.

b. Grandma loves her letter.

Macmillan/McGraw-Hill

128 **Extension:** Have children share a favorite photograph from home. Ask them to tell something about the picture.

Level 7/Unit 1
ORGANIZE INFORMATION: Use Illustrations

SHIP SHAPE

Read what happened first. Then write what might happen next. Use the endings below.

faded and torn.
rose from their beds.
polished and shined them.
was crisp and hard.
rolled and tipped.

1. The wind began to blow and the ship

_____

2. The wind and the sun had made the ship's flag

_____

3. The cook left the roast in the oven too long, so it

_____

4. In the morning when the trumpet blew, the sailors

_____

5. The sailor's black shoes were not shiny, so he

_____

Extension: Have children make up their own ending for this sentence: "The man at the dock untied the ropes and pulled in the anchor as the ship _____ ."

129

WHAT BECAME OF THE MONK(EY)?

Animal Fair

I went to the animal fair;
The birds and the beasts were there.
The big baboon by the light of the moon
Was combing his auburn hair.
You ought to have seen the monk;
He jumped on the elephant's trunk.
The elephant sneezed and fell on his knees,
And what became of the monk?

Read "The Animal Fair." Where does the poem take place?
Write the words in the center circle. Write the name of each
animal in the poem in the other circles.

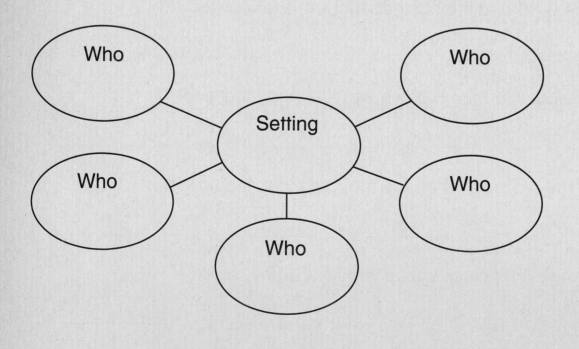

Extension: Have children name other animals that might be found in
the setting described in the poem.

Level 7/Unit 1
ANALYZE STORY ELEMENTS:
Character, Setting

Macmillan/McGraw-Hill

NEW SCHOOL, NEW FRIEND

Imagine that you are a new student. At first you do not have any friends. After a while, you and Pat become good friends.

Write a letter to an old friend. Write about how you felt when you first came to the new school. Then write about how you felt after you got to know Pat.

Dear _____,

    I have been at my new school for two weeks.

At first, I felt _____. When we went out to

play, I _____.

After I met Pat, I felt _____.

Now when I go out to play, _____.

                        Your friend,

                        _____

Macmillan/McGraw-Hill

6

Level 7/Unit 1
ORGANIZE INFORMATION: Comparison and Contrast

Extension: Have children compare and contrast their feelings about a current event at school, a friendship with a classmate, or the arrival or departure of a class pet.

131

SOPHIE'S LETTER

A. Think about "Dear Daddy..." Complete this chart to show where each person in the story can be found.

Person	Where Is He/She?
Mommy	_____
Timmy	_____
Sophie	_____
Daddy	_____

B. Think about "Dear Daddy..." Answer each question. Use a complete sentence.

1. Why couldn't Sophie be with her father?

_____

_____

_____

2. When Sophie could not be with her father, how did she let him know what was happening?

_____

_____

_____

132

Extension: Encourage children to share other ways they might keep in contact with someone who is far away.

Level 7/Unit 1
Story Comprehension

6

Macmillan/McGraw-Hill

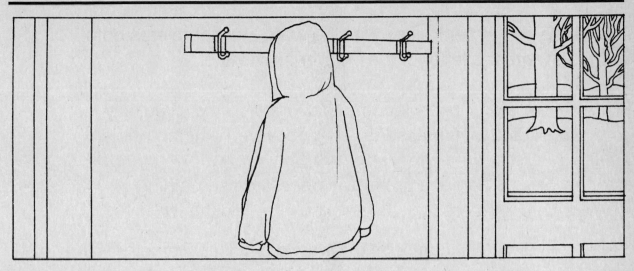

Name: _____   Date: _____

HOOD HOOK

Read each sentence. Underline the word that has the same ending sound as **hood** or **hook**. Write the word on the line.

1. Mommy and I took a walk. _____

2. We wanted to get some wood. _____

3. The wind shook the trees. _____

4. I put on my hood. _____

5. There was ice in the brook. _____

6. I went to look for some fish. _____

7. They were hiding in a nook. _____

8. Soon it would be time to cook. _____

9. We went home to read a book. _____

10. It was good to be together. _____

10

Level 7/Unit 1
Variant Vowels and Phonograms /ù/
-ook, -ood

Extension: Have children write a rhyme, using the words they wrote.

133

Macmillan/McGraw-Hill

BEST WISHES, ED

Match the pair of sentences with the word that completes both of them. Write the letter of the answer on the line.

a. expect **b.** understand **c.** arrows **d.** breaking
e. sliding **f.** message **g.** covered **h.** footprints

_____ 1. When you are moving easily on something, you are _____ . Don't go _____ on the ice.

_____ 2. _____ can point the way to a place. Some _____ mean "go right."

_____ 3. When you think something will happen, you _____ it to happen. If it is cloudy, you _____ rain.

_____ 4. Tracks made by shoes are _____. You can make _____ in the snow.

_____ 5. If something cracks into pieces, it is _____. A crunching noise may be shells _____.

_____ 6. Information that you send or receive is a _____. You can call someone and leave a _____.

_____ 7. If something has something else on top, it is _____. The ground may be _____ with snow.

_____ 8. If you know what something means, you _____ it. You might _____ how to add numbers.

Extension: Have children select three of the words in the box and use them in sentences.

Macmillan/McGraw-Hill

WHALE'S TRAIL

wh**ale**

t**rail**

Read the poems. Underline the words with **ale** or **ail**.
Write the words on the lines.

Before the ship set sail,

The sky was very pale,

Then came a storm of hail,

That left an icy trail.

_____ _____ _____ _____

The sailor told a lively tale

About a gentle, large, white whale,

He wasn't frail; he was quite strong.

Each day he sang a lovely song.

_____ _____

_____ _____

Level 7/Unit 1
Long Vowels and Phonograms
/ā/ -ale, ail

Extension: Have children make up more rhymes with these sounds.

135

Macmillan/McGraw-Hill

WHICH WAY?

Which sentence tells about the picture? Fill in the circle next to the correct answer.

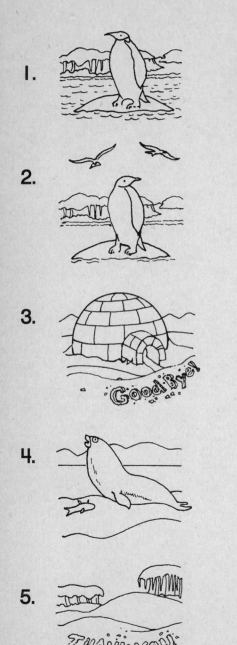

1. ⓐ The penguin is on the island.
   ⓑ The penguin is off the island.

2. ⓐ Terns flew over the penguin.
   ⓑ Terns flew under the penguin.

3. ⓐ A message is in back of the igloo.
   ⓑ A message is in front of the igloo.

4. ⓐ A fish is to the left of the seal.
   ⓑ A fish is to the right of the seal.

5. ⓐ An N is between the A and the K.
   ⓑ An H is between the K and the A.

Macmillan/McGraw-Hill

136 **Extension:** Have pairs of children with a ball demonstrate over, under, in, out, on, off, left, right, between, front, and back.

Level 7/Unit 1
ORGANIZE INFORMATION: Spatial Relationships 5

BATH PATH

path   bath

Write the word from the box that has a different meaning than the underlined word.

thaw	third	thin	earth	thick

I. not <u>second</u>, but _____

2. not <u>sky</u>, but _____

3. not <u>fat</u>, but _____

4. not <u>freeze</u>, but _____

5. not <u>thin</u>, but _____

Macmillan/McGraw-Hill

CATCH OF THE DAY

Read the story. Then, read each sentence below that tells something that happened in the story. Write why each thing happened.

In the spring, penguins pile up rocks to make a nest. Here, the mother lays an egg. The mother and father crowd together to keep the egg warm until it hatches. Then, the mother leaves to catch fish for her baby. When she comes back, it is the father's turn to catch fish. After the baby gets bigger, the father will teach the young one how to swim and dive. Then the baby can catch its own fish.

The penguins pile up rocks.

_____

The mother and father crowd together.

_____

Mother leaves her baby penguin.

_____

Father teaches the baby how to swim and dive.

_____

Extension: Have children tell about a time when they learned to do something new. What happened? Why did it happen?

Macmillan/McGraw-Hill

Level 7/Unit 1
ORGANIZE INFORMATION: Cause and Effect

IN THE ARCTIC

Sometimes things in a story are real. These things could happen in real life. Sometimes things are make-believe. Make-believe things could never happen in real life.

Read the sentences below. Decide if each is real or make-believe. Put a check in the chart.

	REAL	MAKE BELIEVE
1. A penguin lived on an icy island.		
2. A piece of the island broke off.		
3. A whale splashed the animals with its enormous tail.		
4. A seal wrote a message in the snow.		
5. A walrus built a fire to keep warm.		
6. Seals crowded together to keep warm.		
7. A man in a helicopter saved a stranded whale.		
8. A whale gave a penguin a ride.		

8 Level 7/Unit 1
Fantasy and Reality

Extension: Ask children to share something real and something make-believe about a cold climate.

139

Macmillan/McGraw-Hill

Sum It Up

A summary is a short way to tell what something is about.
Read the rhyme that follows.

A. Underline five or six important words in the rhyme, and
write them on the lines.

One, two, three, four, five,
I caught a fish alive!
Why did you let it go?
Because he bit my finger so.
Which finger did he bite?
The little finger on the right.

I. _____   2. _____

3. _____   4. _____

5. _____

B. Write one sentence that tells what the whole rhyme is
about.

_____

_____

_____

_____

_____

Macmillan/McGraw-Hill

QUOTE ME

Think about the story "Best Wishes, Ed." Who said each sentence? Color the answer.

1. "Ernest doesn't even notice penguins."

2. "I guess I will be here the rest of my life."

3. "Could you write something for me?"

4. "I can't fly."

5. "I have other things to do besides give rides to penguins."

Macmillan/McGraw-Hill

⬚5 Level 7/Unit 1
Story Comprehension

Extension: Have children tell at least one other thing each main character said during the story.

141

A NEW BLUE

blue   new

Circle the word that answers the clue. Then write the word.

I. The sea is this color.

_____

dew   blue   threw

2. To eat you do this.

_____

brew   flue   chew

3. It means money is owed.

_____

due   new   clue

4. These are workers on a ship.

_____

crew   glue   blew

5. This is very thin paper.

_____

glue   flew   tissue

Extension: Have children find pictures of words with these vowel sounds.

Macmillan/McGraw-Hill

PUFF...FLASH...BANG!

whistle	driver	warn	horn
enemy	village	lock	danger

Read the words in the box. Read the clues. Write the correct word next to each clue.

1. This person uses a bus to get me to school every day.

   _____

2. There are no tall buildings or traffic jams in a place like this.

   _____

3. A flashing red light or big sign can warn about this.

   _____

4. I do this to call my dog for dinner. _____

5. If a car comes too close to ours, my father may honk this.

   _____

6. I would rather have a friend than this. _____

7. A boat might go through one of these as it travels up a river.

   _____

8. If you get too close to a hot stove, I might do this so you

   don't get burned. _____

Macmillan/McGraw-Hill

8 Level 7/Unit 1
Selection Vocabulary

Extension: Have children make up riddles about things that can give sight and sound signals.

143

THE MAIN FRAME

Read each story. Then read each main idea. Write two details from each story that support the main idea.

> A traffic light tells you to stop and go.
> A flashing light warns of danger ahead.
> Holiday lights are red and green.

Main idea: A light can be a safety signal.

Detail: _____

Detail: _____

> An ant has a pair of antennas on its head.
> Ants work hard to build their nests.
> Ants carry heavy loads of food to their nests.

Main idea: Ants are busy insects.

Detail: _____

Detail: _____

144   **Extension:** Ask children to add one more detail about each main idea.

Level 7/Unit 1
ORGANIZE INFORMATION: Main Idea
and Supporting Details

4

Macmillan/McGraw-Hill

UNUSUAL WORDS

Use the words in the box to complete the crossword puzzle.

| lighthouse   cannon   belfry   siren   lantern   intersection |

Across

1. a loud warning sound

4. part of a tower that holds bells

6. a large gun that is mounted on a stand

Down

2. the place where two roads cross

3. tower with a bright light to guide ships

5. a hanging holder for a light

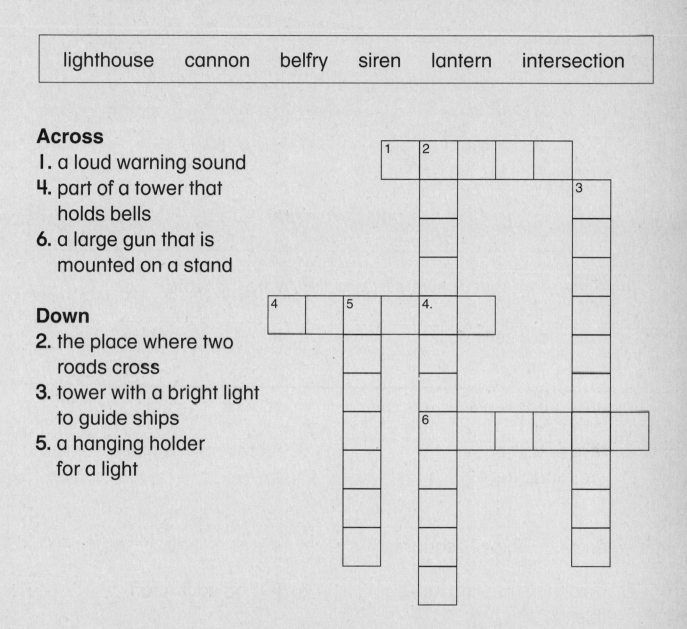

6   Level 7/Unit 1
Unfamiliar Words

Extension: Ask children to make up sentence clues for the words, such as "I heard the (siren) on the police car from far away."

145

Macmillan/McGraw-Hill

A PAIR OF FLARES

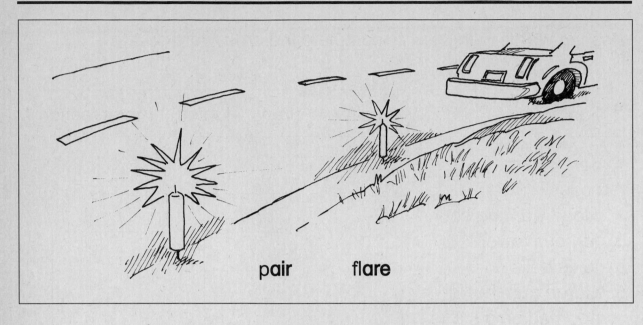

pair   flare

Circle the word that answers the riddle. Write the word.

1. This store sells nails.

_____

beware   hardware   upstairs

2. It has four corners.

_____

square   chair   fare

3. Milk and cheese are made here.

_____

dairy   fair   square

4. A broken watch needs this.

_____

stare   hair   repair

5. Two of something makes this.

_____

spare   pair   hair

6. It is on your head.

_____

fair   chair   hair

Level 7/Unit 1
Variant Vowels and Phonograms /âr/
-are, -air
6

146 **Extension:** Ask children to write a sentence for each word they wrote.

Name: _____ Date: _____

Puff...Flash...Bang!
COMPREHENSION: IMPORTANT AND UNIMPORTANT INFORMATION

WHICH WAY TO THE CLUBHOUSE?

Pretend that you are trying to find your way to your friends' clubhouse in the woods. Read each sentence. Circle YES if it would help you find the clubhouse. Circle NO if the information is not helpful.

1. You have a compass.	YES	NO
2. There are footprints on the path.	YES	NO
3. A sign says "To the Clubhouse."	YES	NO
4. Squirrels are hiding nuts.	YES	NO
5. You remember that the clubhouse is near a pond.	YES	NO
6. Wildflowers along the path are blooming.	YES	NO
7. You hear your friends talking.	YES	NO
8. You see your friends.	YES	NO
9. The sun is setting.	YES	NO
10. Birds are singing.	YES	NO

Macmillan/McGraw-Hill

Extension: Think of an object in the class. Let the children ask 20 questions to gather important information that will help them guess the identity of the object.

WHICH CHICKEN?

whi**ch**   **ch**icken

Write the word that names the picture.

1.

_____

chin   cheese   which

2.

3.

chart   bench   chicken   church   coach   each

4.

5.

church   chain   beach   chair   chill   chain

148   **Extension:** Have children make a rhyme with **ch** words.

Level 7/Unit 1
Consonant Digraphs /ch/ *ch*

5

Macmillan/McGraw-Hill

AS A GENERAL RULE

Read the story. Then read the sentences below the story.
Write YES next to each sentence that is a fact from the story.
Write NO if the sentence is not a fact from the story.

I love summer weather in Texas. It is hot in June, and we go swimming. In July, the temperature may reach 100 degrees. We like to go barefoot in this kind of heat. In August, we start school. We wear shorts and cotton shirts to keep cool.

1. June is a hot month in Texas. _____

2. We can go swimming in June. _____

3. The weather is hot when we start school. _____

4. It is too cool to go barefoot in July. _____

5. It may be 100 degrees in October. _____

Read the sentences in the box. Decide which sentence is a generalization about the story. Write the generalization on the lines.

> Summers are hot in Texas.
> Shorts are good clothes for school.

_____

_____

_____

6 Level 7/Unit 1
Form Generalizations

Extension: Have children write a generalization about how the weather has been in the last week in your city.

149

Macmillan/McGraw-Hill

You Don't Belong

Look at the pictures in each row and read the labels. Color the picture that does not belong.

I.

doorbell   school bell   telephone   refrigerator

2.

railroad crossing   stop sign   library   school zone

3.

cherry   needle   tack   knife

4.

collie   poodle   canary   beagle

Macmillan/McGraw-Hill

150   **Extension:** Have children explain their reasoning to their classmates.

Level 7/Unit 1
ORGANIZE INFORMATION: Categories   4

SIGNALS

Think about "Puff...Flash...Bang!" Complete this chart to show what each signal indicates.

Signal	What Does it Mean?
sirens on a police car	_____
beacon fires	_____
brake lights	_____
lighthouse beacon	_____
checkered flag	_____
American Sign Language	_____
train whistle	_____
Morse code	_____
traffic light	_____
flares	_____

Macmillan/McGraw-Hill

Farm Alarm

farm   cart

Write the word from the box that has the opposite meaning of
the underlined word.

| tart   apart   arm   alarm   harm |

I. not to help, but to _____

2. not together, but _____

3. not sweet, but _____

4. not a leg, but an _____

5. not to calm, but to _____

152

Extension: Have children think of more opposites for other **art** and **arm**
words.

Level 7/Unit 1
Variant Vowels and Phonograms /är/
-art, -arm

5

Macmillan/McGraw-Hill

ANGEL CHILD, DRAGON CHILD

Read the words in the box. Read the incomplete sentences. Write the correct words on the lines to complete the sentences.

pocket	fair	softly	hoping
shoulders	brave	peeked	whispered

1. A girl with hair to her _____ went to the _____ with her friend.

2. She _____ _____ in her friend's ear.

3. They _____ in her big, square _____ and took out some coins.

4. They were _____ they would be _____ enough to try one of the games.

8

Level 7/Unit 1
Selection Vocabulary

Extension: Have children work in pairs or small groups to make up a crossword puzzle, using the selection vocabulary.

153

Macmillan/McGraw-Hill

SING A SILLY SONG

Sing the silly song together. Think about the story the song tells. Then fill in the chart below.

A Peanut Sat on a Railroad Track

A peanut sat on a railroad track,
his heart was all a-flutter,
Round the bend came number ten.
TOOT! TOOT! Peanut butter!

1. Characters (who/what): _____

2. Setting (where): _____

3. What happened first: _____

4. What happened next: _____

5. Ending: _____

Extension: Have children share their favorite story songs. Discuss the characters, setting, and plot of each.

Level 7/Unit 1
ANALYZE STORY ELEMENTS:
Character, Setting, Plot

Macmillan/McGraw-Hill

Name: _____   Date: _____

Angel Child, Dragon Child
PHONICS: Consonant Blends /gl/ *gl*, /fl/ *fl*,
/sl/ *sl*, /bl/ *bl*

BLOSSOM FLOAT

Glistening **bl**ossoms **fl**oated **sl**owly down the stream.

Write the word from the box that has the opposite meaning of the underlined word.

black	slow	flat	asleep	glad

1. not a <u>fast</u> runner, but a _____ one

2. not a <u>white</u> shirt, but a _____ one

3. not <u>awake</u>, but _____

4. not <u>sad</u>, but _____

5. not a <u>bumpy</u> road, but a _____ one

5

Level 7/Unit 1
Consonant Blends /gl/ *gl*, /fl/ *fl*, /sl/ *sl*, /bl/ *bl*   **Extension:** Ask children to think of more **gl**, **fl**, **sl**, and **bl** words.

155

Macmillan/McGraw-Hill

GLUE STEW?

glue   stew

The answer to each riddle has the same ending sound as **stew** or **glue.** Circle the word that answers each riddle. Write the word.

1. The day when homework should be turned in

   _____

   few   amuse   due

2. Something that is not old

   _____

   pew   music   new

3. This is what the plant did.

   _____

   stew   refuse   grew

4. This helps solve a mystery.

   _____

   shoe   clue   crew

5. The color of the sky on a clear day

   _____

   new   yellow   blue

6. What you do when you eat

   _____

   chew   glue   sew

156   **Extension:** Ask children to think of another riddle for one of the **ew** or **ue** words.   Level 7/Unit 1
Variant Vowels and Phonograms /ü /-**ew**, -**ue**

Macmillan/McGraw-Hill

GRANDMA'S LOCKET

Read the first part of the story. Make a guess about the locket and write it on the line. Then read on and see if you were right.

Grandma bought a pretty gold chain. A gold heart hung from it. Grandma held the tiny heart as though it had something very special inside.

1. Guess what was inside the heart locket.

   A jewel was inside.
   Pictures were inside.
   Candy was inside.

Grandma opened the tiny heart and let me look inside.
   "It's Vo-Ding," I said. "You have a picture of my sister in your necklace."
   "Yes," smiled Grandma. "And I have a place for one more picture. Whose picture should I put here?"

2. Guess what Grandma and Chi did next.

   They took Vo-Ding's picture out.
   They read a book.
   They put Chi's picture in the locket.

Extension: If children did not correctly predict what Grandma had inside her locket, ask them to tell why they made the choice they did. Was it reasonable?

Macmillan/McGraw-Hill

RIDDLE ME

Read the riddles. Think about the clues and then write the answers. Use the words in the box.

rainbow

needle

ear

tree

goldfish

1. I have a drum, but it is not for tapping.

I am an _____.

2. I have an eye, but I cannot see.

I am a _____.

3. I have a bark, but I cannot bite.

I am a _____.

4. I am a kind of bow that cannot be tied.

I am a _____.

5. I am covered in gold, but am not worth a lot of money.

I am a _____.

Extension: Challenge children to use clues to create riddles of their own. Record the riddles in a class riddle book.

Macmillan/McGraw-Hill

TWO CLUES

Read the clues. Write the conclusions you reach on the lines.

Clue	Clue	Conclusion
1. Randy rolled the snow into a ball.	Something cold and hard hit Rita.	_____ _____

Clue	Clue	Conclusion
2. Nuong gets a card from Vietnam.	Nuong's dad is away from home.	_____ _____

Clue	Clue	Conclusion
3. The boys call Billy "Carrot Top."	Billy's mom has red hair.	_____ _____

Clue	Clue	Conclusion
4. Jenna's mom buys tickets to get in.	Jenna sees lots of wild animals.	_____ _____

Macmillan/McGraw-Hill

4 Level 7/Unit 1
Draw Conclusions

Extension: Have children think about a pet and create two clues that lead to a conclusion about what the pet is.

159

ANGEL CHILD, DRAGON CHILD

Think about the story "Angel Child, Dragon Child." Picture in your mind's eye the part where the principal tells Hoa and Raymond to help each other. Then answer each question. Use a complete sentence.

1. What happened between Hoa and Raymond right before this part of the story?

   _____

   _____

2. What did Hoa do right after this part of the story?

   _____

   _____

3. Why was this part of the story important?

   _____

   _____

4. How would you describe Hoa and Raymond's feelings both before and after this part of the story?

   _____

   _____

160   **Extension:** Ask children how the story might have ended differently if the principal had not intervened.

Level 7/Unit 1
Story Comprehension   4

Macmillan/McGraw-Hill

TOY JOY

joy   disappoint

Write the word that names the picture.

1.

| soy | voice | toy |

2.

| point | oil | avoid |

3.

| home | coin | joint |

4.

| enjoy | boy | about |

5.

| soil | blue | destroy |

Macmillan/McGraw-Hill

Unit Vocabulary Review

A. Look at each group of words. Listen to your teacher say the words. Underline the word that comes **first** in alphabetical order.

1. covered horn listen	2. breaking lock covered	3. fair village understand	4. footprints expect shoulders
5. peeked hoping ship	6. whistle huge danger	7. whispered warn softly	8. brave except enemy
9. ancient buy message	10. beach castle pocket	11. island bought breaking	12. driver slide hope

B. Look at each group of words. Listen to your teacher say the words. Underline the word that comes last in alphabetical order.

13. whispered understand brave	14. ship sliding footprints	15. village breaking listen	16. expect whistle huge

162   **Extension:** Have children make flash cards for each answer and then arrange the cards in alphabetical order.

Level 7/Unit 1
Unit Vocabulary Review
16

Macmillan/McGraw-Hill

JAMAICA TAG-ALONG

swing	repair	fountain	sneaked
edge	pile	sidewalk	sand

Read the story. Choose a word from the box to complete each sentence. Write the word in the sentence. Then reread the story to check your answers.

The city fixed the broken _____ near the

playground. They used cement to _____ it. A

huge truck dumped a _____ of sand. The

_____ was mixed with lime to make the cement.

Workers poured the cement into a frame. While the cement was still

soft, workers scraped along the sides to make a smooth

_____. Before the cement hardened, a child

_____ up and stepped into it. I still see the

footprint each time I go to _____ at the

playground or go to get a drink from the drinking

_____.

8 Level 7/Unit 2
Selection Vocabulary

Macmillan/McGraw-Hill

Extension: Have children use as many words as they can to make a story.

163

Name: _____ Date: _____

ART THE DARK SHARK

shark

Art

The word that names each picture has the same sound you hear at the beginning of **Art**. Circle the word and write it on the line.

1.   tar   _____
   bat
   jar

2.   arm   _____
   farm
   car

3.   tart   _____
   cart
   pair

4.   car   _____
   cat
   far

5.   shark   _____
   park
   show

164   **Extension**: Ask children to use each word that they wrote in a sentence.

Level 7/Unit 2
Variant Vowels and Phonograms /är/
-ar, -ark, -art, -arm   5

Macmillan/McGraw-Hill

WHAT A WHALE

whale

The word that names each picture has the same beginning sound as **whale**. Circle the word that names each picture. Then write the word.

1.
thistle
when
whistle

_____

2.
whiskers
whether
wish

_____

3.
wait
wheat
what

_____

4.
wheel
which
wall

_____

5.
win
while
whirl

_____

Macmillan/McGraw-Hill

Two Points!

Jim and Jessica were playing basketball. Jim passed the ball to Jessica. Jessica bounced the basketball. Pa-pom, pa-pom, pa-pom. Then, she shot the ball into the air. The ball rolled around the rim and into the basket.
"You made it!" shouted Jim. "Two points!"

What happened when Jim and Jessica played basketball?
Write the events in order.

Jim and Jessica played basketball.

First, Jim _____

_____

Next, Jessica _____

_____

Then, Jessica _____

_____

Last, the ball _____

_____

Extension: Encourage children to describe the ways points are scored in their favorite game or sport. Ask them to use the words *next, then* and *last* to tell the order.

Level 7/Unit 2
ORGANIZE INFORMATION: Sequence of Events

Macmillan/McGraw-Hill

SAND CASTLES

Read each story. Guess what will happen next. Circle your guess. Then write it on the lines.

1. Calvin is building a castle of sand. He scoops water from the ocean to fill the moat. All at once a big wave comes towards the sand castle.

What happens next?

| The castle gets bigger. | The wave hits the castle. | Calvin knocks the castle down. |

_____

_____

2. A hermit crab is too big for his shell. He climbs out of his old home. He runs down the shore. The crab sees a big shell. It is empty and clean.

What happens next?

| The crab digs a hole. | The crab goes back to his old shell. | The crab makes a home in the big shell. |

_____

_____

2 Level 7/Unit 2
Make, Confirm, or Revise Predictions

Extension: Let children begin to tell a story about something that happened to them. Let others try to predict the ending.

167

Macmillan/McGraw-Hill

CHILLY AND PLAYFUL

The play**ful** dog runs in the love**ly** snow.

Write the word from the box that has the opposite meaning of the underlined word. The new word ends in -**ly** or -**ful**.

quietly	careful	sadly	useful	friendly

1. not to be <u>careless</u>, but to be _____

2. not a <u>mean</u> dog, but a _____ one

3. not being <u>loud</u>, but playing _____

4. not <u>happily</u>, but _____

5. not <u>useless</u>, but _____

168 **Extension:** Have children make up sentences using each of the words in the box.

Level 7/Unit 2
STRUCTURAL CLUES: Prefixes and
Suffixes -*ly*, -*ful*   5

Macmillan/McGraw-Hill

Basketball

Read the story. Underline the things Syd will need in order to play basketball. Then, write a sentence that tells the most important ideas in the story.

Syd wants to learn how to play basketball. His dad told Syd that they could put up a basketball hoop at their house. Syd will have to buy a new basketball , as well. His old one has a hole in it. He will need a pump to put air in his new ball. He will also need new sneakers .

Summary:

_____

_____

_____

_____

Macmillan/McGraw-Hill

 5 Level 7/Unit 2
Summarize

Extension: Give a series of oral directions to the class. Then stop and have children summarize what you've said.

169

JAMAICA TAG-ALONG

Think of the things that happened in the story "Jamica Tag-Along." Number the pictures to show the order in which things happened in the story.

☐ Jamaica builds a sand castle.

☐ Berto wants to play, too.

☐ Ossie says, "No."

☐ Jamaica wants to play.

☐ Jamaica says, "No."

☐ Jamaica says, "Yes."

170 **Extension:** Have children retell the story in their own words.

Level 7/Unit 2
Story Comprehension
6

Macmillan/McGraw-Hill

SHOOT HOOPS

The answer to each riddle ends with the same sound as either
shoot or **hoop**. Circle the word that answers each riddle.
Then write the word.

Shoot** through the h**oop**.

I. The sound a train whistle
makes

   hoot
   toot
   foot

_____

2. Something you wear on
each foot in the snow

   boot
   toot
   boat

_____

3. A way to get ice cream
out of the box

   loop
   scoop
   soup

_____

4. Part of a plant

   roof
   coop
   root

_____

5. What will happen to a
plant that does not get
enough water

   droop
   troop
   book

_____

Macmillan/McGraw-Hill

5   Level 7/Unit 2
Variant Vowels and Phonograms /ü/
-oot, -oop

Extension: Have children make up a short story using the circled
words.

171

THE BEST FRIENDS CLUB

Read each sentence. Fill in the circle next to the meaning of the underlined word.

1. She quit her old job when she got another one.
   - ⓐ to begin again
   - ⓑ to stop doing something

2. They are all members of the same family.
   - ⓐ to belong to a group
   - ⓑ team players

3. Schools set up rules for students to follow.
   - ⓐ routes to take
   - ⓑ the right things to do

4. The children promise to work harder in school.
   - ⓐ ask to go somewhere
   - ⓑ agree to something

5. The baby crawled under the table.
   - ⓐ moved on hands and knees
   - ⓑ drew a picture

6. Do you belong to the art club?
   - ⓐ people who meet for a special purpose
   - ⓑ company that sells goods

7. They sit on the front porch to watch the stars.
   - ⓐ part of a car
   - ⓑ part of a house

8. Why were you chasing that cat?
   - ⓐ running after
   - ⓑ catching

Extension: Have children tell the meaning for one of the underlined words. Have other children tell the word being defined.

Macmillan/McGraw-Hill

THE FRIENDS RODE HOME

rode   h**ome**

The answer to each riddle has the same ending sound as
either **rode** or **home**. Circle the word that answers each riddle.
Then write the word.

I. A person in a folktale who lives
   in the earth.

   code   goat   gnome   _____

2. Went on a bicycle.

   rode   walked   dome   _____

3. A secret message.

   sold   code   home   _____

4. A place to live.

   rode   shoe   home   _____

5. A roof that is round.

   dome   some   comb   _____

5

Level 7/Unit 2
Long Vowels and Phonograms *-ome,*
-ode

Extension: Have children use each circled word in a sentence.

173

Macmillan/McGraw-Hill

WHAT KIND OF PERSON

Read the story. Then fill in the chart to tell about Frank.

Frank Wooly loved to ride horses. He practiced every day. One day, Frank's horse threw him to the ground.

"I will not give up!" Frank cried.

He pushed back his thick hair and dusted off his torn jeans. Frank did not give up. He was just eight years old when he won the horse race at the state fair!

PERSON'S NAME: _____

What does he say?

_____

_____

_____

What does he look like?

_____

_____

_____

What does he do?

_____

_____

_____

What do you like about him?

_____

_____

_____

Macmillan/McGraw-Hill

Extension: Let children share their responses to the last question. Encourage them to share things about each other that they admire.

Level 7/Unit 2
ANALYZE STORY ELEMENTS: Character

8

JOBS FOR THE CLUBHOUSE

What job does each child have in the Tree Climbers' Club?
Read the clues and figure it out. Write the names on the
clubhouse sign, and then write the jobs on the lines below.

TREE CLIMBERS' CLUB

President: _____
Vice President: _____
Note Taker: _____ **Kit** _____
Money Keeper: _____

The members of the club are John, Sandy, Roberto, and Kit.

Kit likes to write notes and letters.
Kit's name is the third name on the sign.

She is the _____ .

John's name is after Kit's name.

John is the _____ .

Sandy is not the President.

Sandy is the _____ .

Roberto's name is before Sandy's name on the sign.

Roberto is the _____ .

Level 7/Unit 2
Make Inferences

Extension: Children may enjoy making up similar brainteasers that
require inference skills.

175

Macmillan/McGraw-Hill

PLEASE PLAY

playground

The answer to each riddle has the same beginning sound as **play**.
Circle the word that answers each riddle. Then write the word.

1. The polite way to ask for
something

play
push
please

_____

2. It means to add.

plus
plan
pot

_____

3. A fruit you can eat

pay
plum
place

_____

4. A lamp has this.

plow
push
plug

_____

176   **Extension:** Help children start a word wall of *pl* words.

Level 7/Unit 2
Consonant Blends /pl/ *pl*   4

Macmillan/McGraw-Hill

FRIENDS' VIEW

drew

The word that completes each sentence ends with the same sound as **drew**. Circle the word. Then write the word on the line.

1. There was morning
   _____ on the grass.

   snow
   new
   dew

   _____

2. A bird _____ over the
   tree.

   flew
   fled
   few

   _____

3. My dad _____ the ball
   to me.

   dew
   threw
   tossed

   _____

4. I _____ up the balloons.

   blew
   drew
   popped

   _____

4 Level 7/Unit 2
Variant Vowels and Phonograms /ü/ -ew

Extension: Have children find more words with the same ending sound as *drew* in their books.

177

Macmillan/McGraw-Hill

CLUES AND CONCLUSIONS

Read the clues. Write the conclusions you reach in the boxes.

Clue	Clue	Conclusion
1. Meg swung the bat.	The umpire yelled, "Strike!"	Meg did not _____

Clue	Clue	Conclusion
2. Jenny is in the Friends Club.	Lynn is in the Friends Club.	Jenny and Lynn _____

Clue	Clue	Conclusion
3. Nick blew out the candles on his cake.	Nick opened all the birthday presents.	It is Nick's _____

Clue	Clue	Conclusion
4. It is the weekend.	It is not Sunday.	Today _____

Extension: Have children think about a sport or game and create two clues that lead to a conclusion about the activity.

Level 7/Unit 2
Draw Conclusions

Macmillan/McGraw-Hill

THE BEST FRIENDS CLUB

Think about the story "The Best Friends Club." Then fill in the chart below.

1. Characters (who): _____

_____

2. Problem: _____

_____

3. What happens: _____

_____

4. Outcome: _____

_____

5. Ending: _____

_____

Macmillan/McGraw-Hill

CHALK DRAW

chalk   draw

Write the word from the box that has the opposite meaning of the underlined word. The new word has one of the ending sounds you hear in **chalk** or **draw**.

raw	walk	thaw	talk	claw

1. not to <u>listen</u>, but to _____

2. not <u>cooked</u>, but _____

3. not a <u>hand</u>, but a _____

4. not to <u>freeze</u>, but to _____

5. not to <u>run</u>, but to _____

Macmillan/McGraw-Hill

180 Extension: Have children make up a riddle for each word in the box.

Level 7/Unit 2
Variant Vowels and Phonograms /ô/
-alk, -aw

HAPPY FACE AND SAD FACE

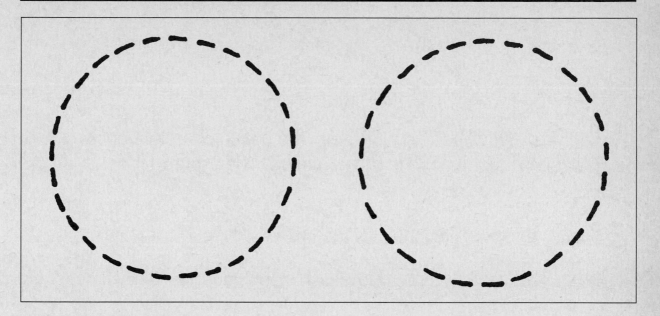

Follow the directions.

1. Trace the dotted lines to make two circles.

2. Write **A** under the circle on the left.
   Write **B** under the circle on the right.

3. Draw two eyes in each circle.
   Draw a nose in each circle.

4. Draw a happy mouth in circle **A**.
   Draw a sad mouth in circle **B**.

5. Draw straight hair on circle **A**.
   Draw curly hair on circle **B**.

6. Draw a hat on circle **A**. Draw stripes on the hat.
   Draw a bow tie on circle **B**. Draw dots on the bow tie.

Macmillan/McGraw-Hill

6 Level 7/Unit 2
Study Skills: Follow Directions

Extension: Have children work in pairs to take turns giving and
following simple oral directions.

181

OUR SOCCER LEAGUE

score	bounce	stretches	charge
pass	tie	touch	field

Read the story. Choose a word from the box to complete each sentence. Write the word in the sentence. Then reread the story to check your answers.

Soccer is a great game to play. Before we play, our team does

_____ to loosen up our muscles. Sometimes,

soccer is hard because you can't _____ the ball

with your hands. Instead, you _____ it to your

teammates using your feet. Other times you _____

it off your head. Our team runs fast down the playing

_____ . My favorite play is when we

_____ the other team as if we mean to attack. We

always try hard to _____ a goal. Sometimes though,

both teams win because the game ends in a _____ .

Teams	1st half	2nd half	Final
Home Team	1	2	3
Visitors	0	3	3

182

Extension: Have children play a game of soccer and then write about it using as many words from the box as possible.

Level 7/Unit 2
Selection Vocabulary

8

WHAT'S THE SCORE?

Teams	1st half	2nd half	Final
Home	O	O	O
Visitors	41	59	100

scoreboard

The word to complete each sentence has the same beginning sounds as **score**. Circle the word. Then write the word in the sentence.

1. A noise can _____ you.

   score   dream   scare

2. Wrap this _____ around your neck.

   scarf   scout   tent

3. I would like a _____ of yogurt.

   scoop   steam   scam

4. You get a _____ after a cut heals.

   scuba   scar   cold

5. Use a _____ to weigh the potatoes.

   stair   score   scale

Level 7/Unit 2
Consonant Blends /sk/ *sc*   **Extension:** Have children write the answers in alphabetical order.   **183**

Macmillan/McGraw-Hill

HERE'S THE SCOOP!

sc**oop**   t**oot**

Underline the words that have the same ending sounds as
toot or **scoop**. Write the words.

1. As we stepped on the tree root,
   the owl made a hoot.
   It scared us so much
   We decided to scoot.

2. As the boat made a loop
   and headed out of the bay,
   Captain Kap put on his boot
   and prepared to sail away.

184 **Extension:** Ask children to write sentences using the underlined words.

Level 7/Unit 2
Variant Vowels and Phonograms
/ü/ *-oot, -oop*   5

Macmillan/McGraw-Hill

THE GOALIE

The coach came over to the goalie box. "We are one point ahead," he said to Judy. "If you can keep the White Socks from scoring a goal, we will win!"

The game started again. The soccer ball was kicked hard. It came right at Judy. She bent down to get the ball, but a White Socks player kicked the ball again. Judy jumped and stretched. She stopped the ball! She also stopped the White Socks from scoring! The game was over. Judy's team won!

Color the circles beside the sentences that tell the most important ideas.

○ Judy had to keep the White Socks from scoring.

○ The White Socks were a good soccer team.

○ Judy stopped the ball.

○ Judy's team won.

Put the main ideas together. Write one or two sentences to tell the most important ideas about the soccer game.

_____

_____

Macmillan/McGraw-Hill

 Level 7/Unit 2
Summarize

Extension: Invite children to summarize events that occur in the classroom, such as games, science experiments, or art explorations.

185

Scoring and Cheering

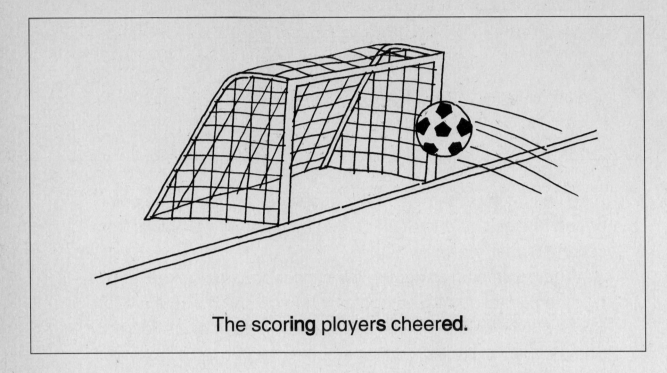

The scor**ing** player**s** cheer**ed**.

Write the word from the box that has the opposite meaning of the underlined word.

resting	friends	throwing	walked	wins

1. not <u>enemies</u>, but _____

2. not <u>catching</u>, but _____

3. did not <u>run</u>, but _____

4. not <u>working</u>, but _____

5. not who <u>loses</u>, but who _____

186   **Extension:** Have children think of more *s, ed, ing* words.

Level 7/Unit 2
Inflectional Endings -*s*, -*ed*, -*ing*
5

Macmillan/McGraw-Hill

PLAY OR PLAY?

The underlined words have more than one meaning. Fill in the circle next to the meaning the underlined word has in the sentence.

1. Melissa likes to <u>play</u> on the swings with her friends.

　ⓐ to have fun

　ⓑ a move or action in a game

2. Brandon made an important <u>play</u> in the soccer game.

　ⓐ to have fun

　ⓑ a move or action in a game

---

3. The store will <u>charge</u> you for the toy.

　ⓐ to rush forward

　ⓑ to ask a price for

4. Jake will <u>charge</u> to the end of the field with the ball.

　ⓐ to rush forward

　ⓑ to ask a price for

---

5. The children will take a <u>break</u> for lunch.

　ⓐ to split into parts

　ⓑ a short rest period

6. The glass will probably <u>break</u> if it falls on the floor.

　ⓐ to split into parts

　ⓑ a short rest period

Macmillan/McGraw-Hill

THE SCOREKEEPER

Read the story. Then write **first, next, then**, and **last** below the sentence to show when Lisa did each thing.

Teams	1st half	2nd half	Final
Tigers	3	2	5
Cubs	2	0	2

Lisa keeps score for the Tigers. Today they are playing the Cubs. In the first half, the Tigers scored 3 goals. The Cubs scored 2 goals. The Tigers played hard during the second half. Jeff scored a goal. Meg kicked a goal, too. Lisa put a 2 on the scoreboard. The whistle blew. The game was over. Lisa counted up the goals. She put the number in the last box. The Tigers won!

Lisa wrote a 5 in the box.

_____

Lisa gave the Tigers a 3.

_____

Lisa gave the Cubs a 2.

_____

The Cubs scored 0 and the Tigers scored 2.

_____

Macmillan/McGraw-Hill

188   **Extension:** Have children tell about common events or activities that involve a sequence, for example, getting dressed or planting a seed.

Level 7/Unit 2
ORGANIZE INFORMATION: Sequence of Events

4

OUR SOCCER LEAGUE

Think about the story "Our Soccer League." Draw pictures to show six things you learned about soccer. Write a label for each picture.

1. _____	**2.** _____
3. _____	**4.** _____
5. _____	**6.** _____

Extension: Invite children who play soccer to demonstrate specific kicks and maneuvers from the story. Encourage all of the children to try them.

189

Macmillan/McGraw-Hill

A Torn Score

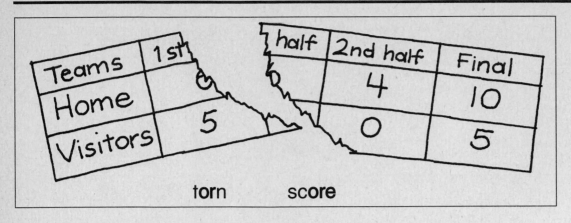

Teams	1st	half	2nd half	Final
Home			4	10
Visitors	5		0	5

torn   score

The name for each picture has the same sound heard in **torn** and **score**. Circle the word that names each picture. Then write the word.

1. star
    store
    story   _____

2. fork
    fern
    for   _____

3. shell
    short
    shore   _____

4. corn
    cork
    comb   _____

5. tore
    ton
    torch   _____

190 **Extension:** Have children use each answer in a sentence.

Level 7/Unit 2
Variant Vowels and Phonograms /ôr/
-or, -ore

5

Macmillan/McGraw-Hill

SOCCER SCORE

	Sharks	Penguins	Ducks	Giants	Bears

Read the graph to find out how many games each soccer team in the league has won. Use the graph to answer each question. Write the answers on the lines.

1. Who won the most games? _____

2. Who won the least number of games? _____

3. Who won three games? _____

4. Who won one more game than the Bears? _____

5. Who won two more games than the Bears? _____

6. Who won three games less than the Giants? _____

6 Level 7/Unit 2
Graphic Aids: Graphs

Extension: With the class use the information on the bar graph to make a pictograph. Use soccer balls for each game won.

191

Macmillan/McGraw-Hill

PRINCESS POOH

allowance	muddy	bottles	perfect
sweet	braces	throne	prize

Read the story. Choose a word from the box to complete each sentence. Write the word in the sentence. Then reread the story to check your answers.

Once upon a time, a young prince was looking for the

_____ princess to marry. He offered a

_____ for anyone who helped him. The first

princess had _____ boots. The prince spent his

_____ on the second princess, but she didn't

even say thank-you. The third princess brought many

_____ of perfume. But the fourth princess, who

had _____ on her teeth and a beautiful,

_____ smile, was just right. She would be the one

to sit on the _____.

Extension: Have children draw a picture of part of the story and use some of the words from the box to tell about it.

Level 7/Unit 2
Selection Vocabulary

Macmillan/McGraw-Hill

WHEN IS IT?

Read the clues. Think about what you know about morning, noon, and night. Then, color the picture that shows when each activity takes place.

1. It is dark.
   The moon is out.
   An owl hoots.

2. Kim goes to lunch.
   The sun is hot.
   There are no shadows.

3. The sun wakes Bill.
   He goes out of the tent.
   Dew is on the grass.

4. The sun goes down.
   It is late.
   Sue closes her bakery.

Macmillan/McGraw-Hill

 Level 7/Unit 2
Make Inferences

Extension: Have children give clues to describe activities they do every day. Have others guess the time of day each activity occurs.

193

DEEP SLEEP

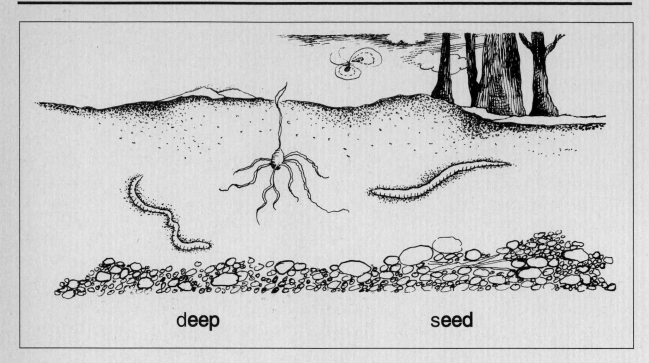

deep   seed

The words in the box have the same ending sounds as **deep** or **seed**. Write the word from the box that has the opposite meaning of the underlined word.

keep	asleep	weed	freed	weep

1. not <u>awake</u>, but _____

2. not <u>locked up</u>, but _____

3. not a <u>rose</u>, but a _____

4. not <u>throw away</u>, but _____

5. not <u>laugh</u>, but _____

194 **Extension:** Have children write a short story using the words in the box.

Level 7/Unit 2
Long Vowels and Phonograms: /ē/
-eep, -eed 5

A ROYAL THRONE

throne

The word that completes each sentence begins with the same beginning sound as **throne.** Circle the word that completes each sentence. Then write the word.

1. The number after two is _____.

   thrill   three   threat

2. A pitcher _____ the ball.

   throws   thrash   thrive

3. You need _____ to sew a dress.

   threw   thrush   thread

4. Sometimes you get a sore _____ with a cold.

   thrift   throat   thrown

5. A princess sits on a small _____ .

   through   thrive   throne

Macmillan/McGraw-Hill

Almost the Same

Read the sentences. Look for other words that mean about the same thing as the underlined word. Then color in the circle next to the definition.

1. Grandma has jars, cans, and <u>bottles</u> full of apple juice.

   ⓐ containers made of glass

   ⓑ kind of fruit

2. Luke wears metal <u>braces</u> on his legs.

   ⓐ something that makes a body part stronger

   ⓑ something that smells strong

3. Tim's face was dirty and his wet feet were <u>muddy</u>.

   ⓐ covered with paint

   ⓑ filled with dirt and mud

4. Meg won a blue ribbon, but Ned's <u>prize</u> was a star.

   ⓐ something you win

   ⓑ something you see at night

5. The king sat on a <u>throne</u>. The prince sat on an old chair.

   ⓐ fancy chair used by a king

   ⓑ something you dive off of into the water

196

Extension: Make a list of unfamiliar words as children encounter them. Have children write one or more synonyms for the words to help them remember what each word means.

Level 7/Unit 2
Context Clues: Unfamiliar Words

5

Macmillan/McGraw-Hill

CARNIVAL GAMES

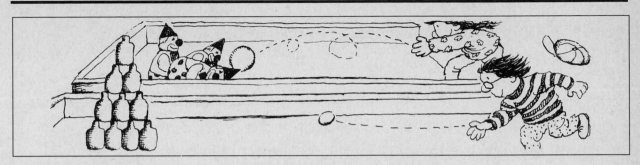

Bottle Ball
3 balls for 50 cents
Get all 10 bottles down
and you WIN!

Clowns Down
3 balls for 50 cents
Knock all 3 clowns over
and you WIN!

Think about how the carnival games are alike. Think about how they are different. Write your ideas on the chart.

ALIKE	DIFFERENT
_____	_____
_____	_____
_____	_____
_____	_____
_____	_____
_____	_____

Macmillan/McGraw-Hill

Level 7/Unit 2
Organize Information: Comparison and Contrast

Extension: Children may compare and contrast some of their favorite games.

Laundry Lady

Read the story about Mrs. Tibbs. Then fill in the web below to tell about Mrs. Tibbs.

    Mrs. Tibbs owns a laundry. People bring their dirty clothes to her. She washes the clothes. She dries the clothes and folds them, too. Mr. Wo loves to bring his clothes to her. He says Mrs. Tibbs does the best job in town. "She is happy. I love to hear her sing so sweetly while she works!" says Mr. Wo. "And nobody gets clothes cleaner!"

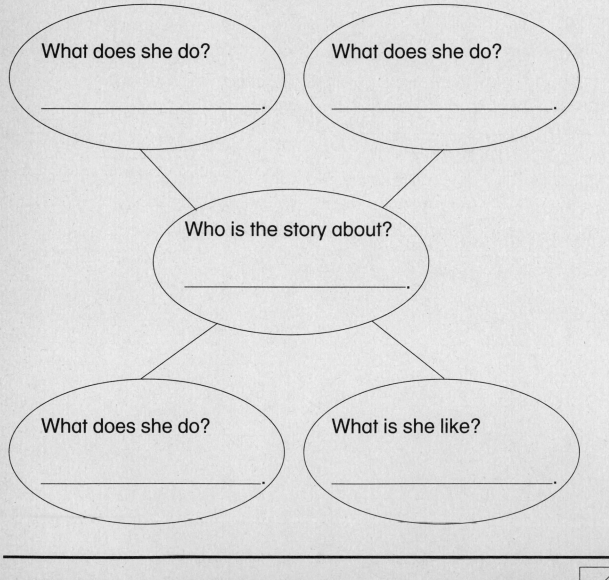

What does she do?
_____.

What does she do?
_____.

Who is the story about?
_____.

What does she do?
_____.

What is she like?
_____.

Extension: Invite children to share things they think Mrs. Tibbs might say. Ask them to tell why they think she would say those things.

Level 7/Unit 2
Character, Plot

Macmillan/McGraw-Hill

USE CLUES

Read the clues. Write what you think the clues mean under the word **conclusion**.

Clue	Clue	Conclusion
1. Tia sees a black and white animal.	It squirts something very stinky.	_____ _____

Clue	Clue	Conclusion
2. Kate can see over the fence.	Her pants are never long enough.	_____ _____

Clue	Clue	Conclusion
3. Buck never puts his toys away.	His bed is not made.	_____ _____

Clue	Clue	Conclusion
4. Mom has worked hard all day.	Mom is yawning.	_____ _____

4 Level 7/Unit 2
Draw Conclusions

Extension: Have children make up clues about a story character. Have classmates guess who the story character is.

199

Macmillan/McGraw-Hill

PRINCESS POOH

Think about "Princess Pooh." Draw a line to match the beginning of each sentence with the end.

I. Princess Pooh   says Penelope is wonderful.

2. Patty Jean Piper   is jealous of her sister.

3. Grandma   must sit in a wheelchair.

4. Dad   carries Princess Pooh's
                                    throne in his car.

5. Carnival Man   takes Princess Pooh to therapy.

6. Mom   gives Penelope a prize.

Extension: Ask children to tell how Patty Jean felt about her sister at the beginning of the story and then at the end. What made her change her mind?

200

Level 7/Unit 2
Story Comprehension
6

Macmillan/McGraw-Hill

ROW ALONG THE COAST

row   coast

The word that names each picture below has the same sound you hear in **row** and **coast**. Circle the word that names each picture. Then write the word on the line.

1.

roast   root   row   _____

2.

cloud   coast   crow   _____

3.

alone   apple   arrow   _____

4.

tow   toast   taste   _____

4

Level 7/Unit 2
Long Vowels and Phonograms: /ō/
-*oast, -ow*

Extension: Ask children to think of more words with the same ending sounds as *row* and *coast*.

201

Macmillan/McGraw-Hill

UNIT VOCABULARY REVIEW

Look at the words in each group. Underline the word your teacher says.

1. swing sand sweet	**2.** chasing charge covered	**3.** bounce bottles bought	**4.** streams stretches slide
5. whistle rules tails	**6.** huge quit queen	**7.** crawled carried curve	**8.** softly string swing
9. tie touch throne	**10.** braces breaking brave	**11.** garage president repair	**12.** team allowance battle
13. prize pass promise	**14.** either earth edge	**15.** members many muddy	**16.** perfect pile porch
17. sneaked sidewalk score	**18.** forever finish fountain	**19.** castle club curly	**20.** field forest forget

Extension: Have each child look up a different word in the dictionary to find its meaning. Students can share the words and their meanings.

Level 7/Unit 2
Unit Vocabulary Review

Macmillan/McGraw-Hill

COME A TIDE

piano	radios	creeks	mountains
tide	flood	river	neighbor

Read the words in the box. Read the incomplete sentences.
Write the word that completes each sentence.

1. Many people listen to the news on their _____ .

2. The heavy rains caused a _____ .

3. The skiers were happy to hear it was snowing in the

   _____ .

4. Large boats were traveling down the _____ on

   their way to the ocean.

5. My mother makes beautiful music when she plays the

   _____ .

6. My next door _____ has a leak in her roof.

7. Many little _____ flowed into the river.

8. The ocean _____ rises and falls about

   twice a day.

 Level 7/Unit 3
Selection Vocabulary

Extension: Invite children to choose one sentence to copy and
illustrate.

203

A GOOD BOOK

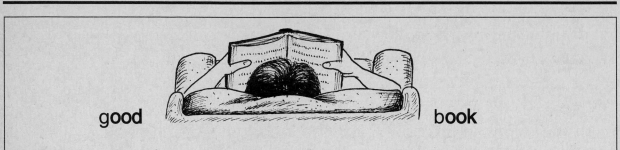

good   book

The answer to each riddle has the same ending sound as **good** or **book**. Circle the word that answers each riddle. Then write the word on the line.

1. It is a place to hang a coat.   _____

    hook   snap   look

2. This comes from trees.   _____

    flood   food   wood

3. An earthquake did this.   _____

    took   shook   shone

4. You do this to raw fish.   _____

    cook   fool   book

5. Something that goes on your head.   _____

    This   hood   mud

204   **Extension:** Have children write a sentence with **good** and **book**.

Level 7/Unit 3
Variant Vowels and Phonograms /ü/
-ood, -ook   5

Macmillan/McGraw-Hill

GRANDMA'S BISCUITS

Read the story about Grandma's biscuits. Think about what happened and why it happened.

"It's too lumpy," Grandma grumbled to Ellen. She mixed in more water. Then she rolled out the dough on the table. "I like my biscuits the same size. Get me a glass," said Grandma. She turned the glass upside down to cut the biscuits. Then she put the tray in the oven to bake. In twelve minutes the bell rang. Guess who was first in line? Ellen was!

Read each cause. Then write its effect.

Cause	Effect
The dough was too lumpy.	_____ _____
Grandma likes her biscuits the same size.	_____ _____
The biscuits had to bake.	_____ _____
Ellen liked hot biscuits.	_____

 4 Level 7/Unit 3
Organize Information: Cause and Effect

Extension: Ask children to name some events that have happened in the classroom. Have them suggest probable causes for each event.

205

Macmillan/McGraw-Hill

CREEKS AND RIVERS

The only way to get to John's cabin is by boat. When we go
to John's cabin, we put our boat in Lake Sunrise. We paddle
across the lake. Then we travel down Red River. We pass
many little creeks. Dad knows the creek that leads to the cabin.
A dead oak tree hangs over it. John calls it Duck Soup Creek.
We paddle under the tree limb. We can see the cabin.

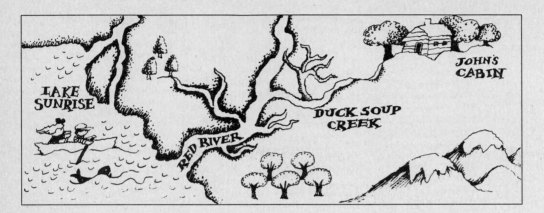

A. Write the name of each body of water in the story.

_____

_____

_____

B. Write one sentence that tells what the whole story is about.

_____

_____

_____

Extension: Let children share trips they have taken. Encourage them to
summarize the experience in one or two sentences.

Level 7/Unit 3
Summarize

4

Macmillan/McGraw-Hill

DOCTOR FOSTER

A. Read the rhyme aloud. Think about what happens when
Doctor Foster goes on a trip.

Doctor Foster went to Gloucester
In a shower of rain;
He stepped in a puddle,
Right up to his middle,
And he never went there again.

B. Write the events in order.

First, Doctor Foster _____.

Next, it _____.

Then, Doctor Foster _____.

Last, he _____.

4

Level 7/Unit 3
**Organize Information: Sequence of
Events**

Extension: Have children describe the sequence of events they follow
to get to school in the morning.

207

Macmillan/McGraw-Hill

IT'S GOING TO RAIN

Read the story. Look for words that do not mean exactly what they say. Then complete the chart below.

Jamie walked to the bus stop. The sky turned dark, and the rain began to fall. At first, it just sprinkled. The bus stopped. The driver honked. "Hurry, Jamie. We've got to hit the road!" Soon they came to the fork in the road. By this time, it was raining cats and dogs. It was hard to see out the window. Luckily, the driver knew which way to go.

	What pictures do the words make you think of?	What do the words really mean?
"hit the road"		
"fork in the road"		
"raining cats and dogs"		

208 **Extension:** Make a list of other favorite expressions. Let children tell what they mean.

Level 7/Unit 3
Context Clues: Figurative Language

6

Macmillan/McGraw-Hill

SNATCH A SNOWFLAKE

snatch   **sn**owflake

The words in the box all begin with **sn**. Choose the word that completes each sentence. Then write the word.

snack	sneeze	sniffs	snake	snug

1. The _____ moved through the grass.

2. Crackers and cheese make a good _____ .

3. Dust sometimes makes me _____ .

4. The soft pillow and warm blanket made a _____ bed.

5. My dog puts her nose in the air and _____ .

Macmillan/McGraw-Hill

5 | Level 7/Unit 3
Consonant Blends /sn/ *sn*

Extension: Have children write a rhyme using words that have the same beginning sound as *snowflake*.

209

COME A TIDE

A. Think about "Come a Tide." Complete this chart to show why each person did not go with Mama.

PEOPLE IN THE STORY	REASON
Joe	_____
Mrs. Mac	_____
the Cains	_____
Papa Bill	_____
	_____

B. Think about "Come a Tide." Answer each question. Use a complete sentence.

1. Why are Mama, Papa, and their family going to Grandma's house?

_____

2. The people in this story are making the best of a bad situation. Write about how the people in the story work together.

_____

_____

_____

Extension: This story is based on real events. Encourage children to list real events in their writing journals that might make interesting stories.

210

Level 7/Unit 3
Story Comprehension

Macmillan/McGraw-Hill

GET OUT OF YOUR HOUSE

out   h**ouse**

The word that completes each sentence has the same ending sound as **out** or **house**. Circle the word to complete each sentence. Then write it on the line.

1. My story is _____ a flood.   _____

   tide   out   about

2. The _____ came in from the field.   _____

   mouse   shout   deer

3. The child was sad and started   _____
   to _____.

   pout   joke   about

4. I bought a new _____ to wear.   _____

   whistle   blouse   house

5. We had to _____ to be heard.   _____

   drive   spout   shout

Level 7/Unit 3
Diphthongs and Phonograms /ou/ *-out,*
-ouse   **Extension:** Have children write the words they circled in alphabetical order.   **211**

Macmillan/McGraw-Hill

THE SUN, THE WIND AND THE RAIN

Match each clue with the correct word. Write the letter of the answer on the line.

_____ 1. A dog or the wind might have done this.

_____ 2. It's the opposite of "smooth and gentle."

_____ 3. It's the opposite of "rough and lumpy."

_____ 4. These can come together to form a river.

_____ 5. Rivers often run through these.

_____ 6. This wind whispers but never howls.

_____ 7. This can mean "not fancy" or "flat land."

_____ 8. Storms can be this way, and so can a wild river.

a. streams

b. plain

c. howled

d. valleys

e. smooth

f. raging

g. breeze

h. rough

212 Extension: Have children use the clues to help them write sentences that use the words.

Level 7/Unit 3
Selection Vocabulary

8

Macmillan/McGraw-Hill

Name: _____   Date: _____

ALIKE AND DIFFERENT

Read each object name. Answer the questions about each object to complete the chart. Write **Y** for **yes**. Write **N** for **no**.

A.

Is it	white?	round?	food?	fun?	hard?
baseball	_____	_____	_____	_____	_____
onion	_____	_____	_____	_____	_____
snowball	_____	_____	_____	_____	_____
soap bubble	_____	_____	_____	_____	_____

B. Use the completed chart to think about how the objects are alike and how they are different.

I. In what way are all 5 objects alike?

_____

2. In what ways is the soap bubble different from the other objects?

_____

_____

22

Level 7/Unit 3
ORGANIZE INFORMATION: Comparison and Contrast

Extension: Challenge children to add one more question to the chart. How do the objects compare using this new trait?

213

Macmillan/McGraw-Hill

Name: _____ Date: _____

SKYLINE AT NIGHT

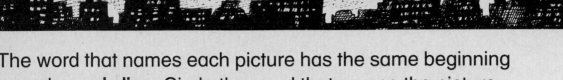

The word that names each picture has the same beginning sounds as **skyline**. Circle the word that names the picture. Write the word on the line.

1. sky   skate   spy   _____

2. sea   skit   ski   _____

3. skunk   shrink   skirt   _____

4. shirt   skirt   skip   _____

5. skate   step   skill   _____

GRACEFUL GEESE

Write the word from the box that has the opposite meaning of the underlined word.

powerful	softly	joyful	countless	spotless

1. not a few stars, but _____

2. not to be weak, but to be _____

3. not dirty, but _____

4. not sad, but _____

5. not to sing loudly, but to sing _____

5

Level 7/Unit 3
Suffixes: *-ful, -ly, -less*

Extension: Have children help make a list of other *-ful, -ly,* and *-less* words.

215

Macmillan/McGraw-Hill

SPIKE AND IKE

Read the story about Spike and Ike. Then answer the
questions that follow.

Spike is Ryan's dog. Ike is his cat. Spike chased Ike up a tree.
Spike chased a squirrel up the tree, too. Ryan had to get Ike
down. Ryan put Spike on a leash after he chased the mail carrier.
But that didn't stop Spike. He barked at the birds and tried to
chase them into the next yard.

What are the facts?

Spike chased _____

Spike chased _____

Spike chased _____

Spike chased _____

What could you say about Spike that is nearly always true?

_____

_____

216

Extension: Have children think about the actions of other pets, such as
cats, birds, or hamsters. Have them make a generalization about each
animal's behavior.

Level 7/Unit 3
Form Generalizations

5

Macmillan/McGraw-Hill

MOUNTAIN CLIMBING

A. How do people climb mountains ?
Here is a list that shows what one climber does.

1. Get a buddy.   **2.** Check gear.

3. Climb as far as I can.   **4.** Toss rope over a rock.

5. Pull myself up.   **6.** Rest at the top.

B. Think about how you do something. Write the steps.
You may want to tell about:

   • How to cut a paper heart   • How to play a game

   • How to make a bed   • How to cook something

How to _____.

1. _____

2. _____

3. _____

4. _____

Macmillan/McGraw-Hill

5   Level 7/Unit 3
Organize Information: Steps in a Process

Extension: Have volunteers read the steps they wrote on this page.
Invite others to guess the activity.

217

COASTING IN THE SNOW

coast   snow

Circle the word that has the same sound as **coast** or **snow**. Then write the word to complete the sentence.

1. The wind began to _____ .

   stop   blow   howl

2. I like to eat jam and _____ .

   show   bread   toast

3. Early in the morning the sun is _____ .

   low   red   snow

4. Mom fixed a _____ turkey for dinner.

   thin   coast   roast

5. We had to _____ to make the boat move.

   row   rough   roast

218   **Extension:** Have children write words that rhyme with *coast* and *snow*.

Level 7/Unit 3
**Long Vowels and Phonograms: /ō/-*ow*,
-*oast***   5

Macmillan/McGraw-Hill

THE SUN, THE WIND AND THE RAIN

Think about "The Sun, the Wind and the Rain." In what ways are the earth mountain and Elizabeth's mountain alike? How are they different? Complete the chart to compare the two mountains.

	earth mountain	Elizabeth's mountain
Formed when?	long ago	_____
Made of what?	rocks	_____
How big?	_____	as tall as a child
Rain does what?	_____ _____	destroys it and carries it to sea

Why do you think the author wrote about the two kinds of mountains? Circle your answer.

- To show how big they are.

- To show mountain canyons.

- To show how mountains change over time.

5

Level 7/Unit 3
Story Comprehension

Extension: Children may enjoy sharing experiences they have had at the beach or the mountains. Encourage them to focus on the sights and sounds.

219

Macmillan/McGraw-Hill

Name: _____ Date: _____

The Sun, the Wind, and the Rain
PHONICS: Long Vowels and Phonograms /e/
-eat, -eak

Neat Peaks

The answer to each riddle has the same ending sound as **neat** or **peak**. Circle the word that answers each riddle. Then write the word.

_____

1. This is what you get on Halloween.

   heat   trout   treat

_____

2. This grain grows in a field.

   wheat   what   weak

_____

3. This is what a clean room is.

   next   neat   cheat

_____

4. This is what you do when you talk.

   speak   seat   spoil

_____

5. This means not strong.

   tease   weak   treat

220 **Extension:** Have children make up a story using the words they circled.

Level 7/Unit 3
Long Vowels and Phonograms /e/ -eat,
-eak

5

Macmillan/McGraw-Hill

CONTEST APPLICATION

If you enter a contest, you may have to fill out an application. Read the application below. Then fill it out with the correct information.

Contest: Sand Castle Building

Date of Contest: July 25, 1997

Name: _____
　　　　　First　　　　　　　　　　　　Last

Today's date: _____

Birth Date: _____

Street Address: _____

City: _____　State: _____

Zip: _____　Phone Number: _____

8

Level 7/Unit 3
**Study Skills: Complete Forms and
Applications**

Extension: Have children write about a contest they have entered or
would like to enter.

221

Macmillan/McGraw-Hill

LLAMA AND THE GREAT FLOOD

point	meadow	language	enough
frightened	thin	during	gathered

Read the story. Choose a word from the box to complete each sentence. Write the word. Then reread the story to check your answers.

The mountain animals were afraid. In fact, they were very

_____ . They _____ in a

grassy _____ . The wise old Alpaca spoke to

them in a _____ they could all understand.

"The grass has become very _____ . The main

_____ is there is very little grass. There may not

be _____ for us all to eat. We must eat only what

we need _____ the next few weeks." All the

animals agreed to work together.

222   **Extension:** Have children write a sentence for each word in the box.

Level 7/Unit 3
Selection Vocabulary   8

Name: _____ Date: _____

Llama and the Great Flood
PHONICS: Diphthongs and Phonograms
/oi/ -oint, -oy

POINT TO JOY

The word that completes each sentence has the same ending sound as **point** or **joy**. Circle the word. Then write the word.

I. A flood can _____ homes.   _____

   point   save   destroy

2. Your elbow forms a _____ .   _____

   joint   joy   part

3. The red train is a _____ .   _____

   spoil   toy   boat

4. A sharp pencil has a _____ at the end.   _____

   point   choice   rolls

5. The baby _____ was in a blanket.   _____

   noise   bunny   boy

5

Level 7/Unit 3
**Diphthongs and Phonograms /oi/ -oint,
-oy**

Extension: Have children write a rhyme using the circled words.

223

Macmillan/McGraw-Hill

FLOOD FLIGHT

The word that answers each riddle has the same beginning sound as **flood** and **flight**. Choose the word that answers the riddle. Write the word.

| flea | float | flat | floor | flour |

1. A cook uses _____ to make bread.

2. The opposite of hilly is _____ .

3. A tiny pest that bites cats and dogs is a _____ .

4. A room has walls, a ceiling, and a _____ .

5. Something that will not sink will _____ .

Extension: Have children write more *fl* words on cards to add to a word wall.

Macmillan/McGraw-Hill

IT'S A LLAMA'S LIFE

Match the beginning of each sentence with its ending. Write
the letter of the answer on the line.

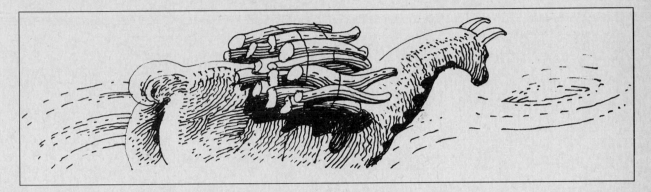

1. Llamas may refuse to move _____

2. Llamas are used to carrying heavy loads _____

3. Llamas stay warm _____

4. Llamas may spit at you _____

5. Llamas don't drink much water _____

a. because they are angry.

b. because they are strong animals.

c. because they get water from plants.

d. because they are stubborn.

e. because they have thick hair.

Macmillan/McGraw-Hill

5

Level 7/Unit 3
**ORGANIZE INFORMATION: Cause and
Effect**

Extension: Have children write one of the sentences that was formed
when the beginning of the sentence was matched with its ending. Then
have them draw a picture to illustrate that sentence.

225

GROUP IT

Read the group names. Then read the words. Group the words by writing each word on a line under its group name.

mountain	joy	potato	valley
pumpkin	island	macaw	anger
fox	corn	meadow	worry
squash	llama	armadillo	sadness

Animals

_____

_____

_____

_____

Land Forms

_____

_____

_____

_____

Foods

_____

_____

_____

Feelings

_____

_____

_____

226   **Extension:** Have children add one word of their choice to each group.

Level 7/Unit 3
ORGANIZE INFORMATION: Categories   16

Macmillan/McGraw-Hill

HOME BUILDERS

Read the story. Write **first** below the picture that shows what happened first. Write **last** below the picture that shows what happened last.

1. The people built new homes. They gathered large stones. They stacked the stones and put clay between them. They made a straw roof to cover the house.

_____   _____

2. The Indians wanted to plant crops on the mountain. Chief Koto put his tools on the llama's back. Running Stream used the tools to plow the dirt and rocks. Little Fox planted the corn and potatoes.

_____   _____

 Level 7/Unit 3
ORGANIZE INFORMATION: Sequence of Events

Extension: Have children describe an event such as visiting relatives. Instruct them to use the words *first, next,* and *last.*

227

Macmillan/McGraw-Hill

THE ELEPHANT'S BAD DAY

A summary is a short way to tell what something is about.
Read the rhyme that follows.

A. Underline five words in the rhyme that you could use to
help you retell the rhyme.

Way Down South
(Anonymous)

Way down South where bananas grow,

A grasshopper stepped on an elephant's toe .

The elephant said, with tears in his eyes,

"Pick on somebody your own size."

B. Write one sentence that tells what the whole rhyme is
about.

_____

_____

_____

_____

Extension: Invite children to make up a class story about a bad day.
Then have children summarize the class story.

Level 7/Unit 3
Summarize

6

Macmillan/McGraw-Hill

READ ALL ABOUT IT!

Write a newspaper article to tell about "Llama and the Great Flood."

Headline: _____

_____

What happened?

_____

_____

_____

_____

Who was involved?

_____

_____

When did it happen?

_____

Where did it happen?

_____

_____

Draw a picture of the event.

Macmillan/McGraw-Hill

Extension: Ask children to follow the format on this page to write a newspaper article about a current event such as a rainstorm or snowstorm.

Name: _____ Date: _____

Llama and the Great Flood
PHONICS: Long Vowels and Phonograms /ā/
-afe, -ave, -aze

A Safe Cave

The word that completes each sentence has the ending sound heard in **safe**, **cave**, or **blaze**. Circle the word that completes each sentence. Then write the word.

1. A _____ is a kind of puzzle.

   story   maze   cave

2. The man with a beard wants to _____.

   safe   show   shave

3. The banker keeps money in a _____.

   haze   safe   cake

4. Fresh fruit is something we _____.

   blaze   crave   spill

5. She awoke in a _____.

   daze   sleep   wave

230 **Extension:** Have students put the answers in alphabetical order.

Level 7/Unit 3
Long Vowels and Phonograms /ā/ -afe,
-ave, -aze   5

Macmillan/McGraw-Hill

A CURVE IN THE RIVER

chance	supposed	floated	travel
strangers	sail	splashed	solid

Read the story. Choose a word from the box to complete each sentence. Write the word in the sentence. Then reread the story to check your answers.

I like to vacation with my parents. Since my dad likes to

_____, we pull our boat on a trailer attached

to the car. We _____ to places where there

is lake. Last year we went to Crystal Lake. My sister and I

swam. We _____ on rafts in the lake.

We _____ water at each other. I even

got a _____ to ride on a jet ski. We also

walked along the lake and looked for shells. One day I found a

_____ gold coin! The children who stayed

in other tents along the lake were _____ at

first. Later they became good friends. We are

_____ to go back to Crystal Lake next year.

I can't wait!

Macmillan/McGraw-Hill

 Level 7/Unit 3
Selection Vocabulary

Extension: Have children act out this story using gestures and expression.

231

It Couldn't Happen!

Read the story. Draw two scenes from the story to show something that could not have happened in real life. Then complete the sentences.

Why Bears Have Short Tails

It was winter and Bear was hungry. Fox led him to a hole in the ice. The hole was filled with fish. Fox told Bear to stick his long tail into the hole. "Fish will bite your tail. When you feel them, pull up your tail. The fish will hang on." Bear waited and waited. He never felt a bite. After a long time, he stood up. When he took his frozen tail out of the water, it snapped and fell off. And that is why bears have short tails.

This is not realistic because   This is not realistic because

_____   _____

_____   _____

_____   _____

_____   _____

Extension: Invite interested children to write a fantasy in which they are the main character.

Level 7/Unit 3
Fantasy and Reality

4

Macmillan/McGraw-Hill

DID IT HAPPEN?

Read the story. Think about what might happen.

> Tony put his toy sailboat in the river. The soft wind pushed the little boat downstream. It went around the bend.
> The wind blew harder and made the water choppy.
> Soon, the boat passed a boy in a real sailboat.
> The toy sailed on toward the mouth of the ocean.
> The sky was dark. The waves were big and white.

A. Write what you think will happen.

_____

_____

B. Read more of the story. Answer the question.

> The boy saw the toy boat. It was bouncing up and down in the river. "I must get that little boat," he said. So he turned his sails. The wind blew him to the toy. He picked up the boat.

What do you think will happen next?

_____

_____

Extension: Ask children to explain why they predicted the ending they did. After discussion, ask if any children would like to revise their original predictions.

Macmillan/McGraw-Hill

A SPECIAL SPOT

The word that completes each idea has the same beginning sound as **special** and **spot**. Choose the word from the box.

spotted	speedy	spend	Speak	space

1. _____ up and say what you want.

2. A _____ car is not a slow one.

3. The rocket flew into _____.

4. I enjoy playing with my _____ cat.

5. I want to _____ money and buy my friend a present.

234   **Extension:** Have each child write a bottle message using *sp* words.

Level 7/Unit 3
Consonant Blends /sp/ *sp*   5

Macmillan/McGraw-Hill

Name: _____ Date: _____

A Curve in the River
PHONICS: Long Vowels and Phonograms /ā/
-afe, -ave, -aze

A Maze!

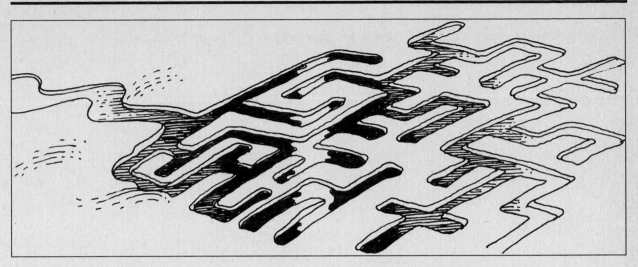

The answer to each riddle has the same ending sound as
safe, **rave**, or **glaze**. Circle the word that answers each riddle.
Write the word.

1. A reason to use a bank. _____

shave   save   soap

2. A campfire can do this. _____

blaze   wood   brave

3. Something you see at the beach. _____

maze   bridge   wave

4. A place to keep treasures. _____

safe   bottle   shave

5. How you feel if you are not afraid. _____

blaze   shy   brave

Macmillan/McGraw-Hill

A CURVE IN THE RIVER

Think about the story "A Curve in the River." Then summarize the story by completing the chart.

Main Character _____

Wanted _____

_____

_____

But (problem) _____

_____

_____

So (solution) _____

_____

_____

_____

Macmillan/McGraw-Hill

236 **Extension:** Have children suggest what will happen to the bottles now.

Level 7/Unit 3
Story Comprehension

4

Name: _____ Date: _____

A Curve in the River
PHONICS: DIPHTHONGS AND PHONOGRAMS
/ou/ -ound, -ow, -own

CLOWN AROUND NOW

The word that names each picture has the same ending sound as **clown, around,** or **now**.

1.

horse   hound   how   _____

2.

cow   clown   creek   _____

3.

crowd   cook   crown   _____

4.

frown   bird   bow   _____

5.

tide   town   sound   _____

Level 7/Unit 3
Diphthongs and Phonograms /ou/ -ound, -ow, -own   **Extension:** Have children make rhymes with words that sound like **clown, around,** and **now.**   **237**

5

Macmillan/McGraw-Hill

UNIT VOCABULARY REVIEW

A. Look at each group of words. Listen to your teacher say the words. Underline the word that comes **first** in alphabetical order.

1. valleys creeks chance	**2.** chance enough breeze	**3.** neighbor howled strangers	**4.** gathered during creeks
5. radios rough raging	**6.** streams supposed travel	**7.** sail splashed smooth	**8.** mountains morning meadow
9. splashed tide thin	**10.** flood gathered frightened	**11.** piano point plain	**12.** language flood enough

B. Write these words in alphabetical order.

solid   valleys   supposed   river

_____

_____

_____

Extension: Have each child look up a different word in the dictionary to find its meaning. Students can share the words and their meanings.

Macmillan/McGraw-Hill